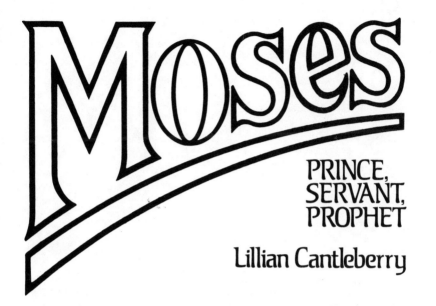

Moses

PRINCE, SERVANT, PROPHET

Lillian Cantleberry

Publishing House
St. Louis

Quotations from the Five Books of Moses, the Psalm of Moses (Psalm 90), and references in the New Testament to Moses are from The Holy Bible: NEW INTERNATIONAL VERSION, © 1978 by the International Bible Society. Used by permission of Zondervan Bible Publishers.

Library of Congress Cataloging in Publication Data

Cantleberry, Lillian, 1922–
    Moses, prince, servant, prophet.

    1. Moses (Biblical leader)—Fiction. I. Title.
PS3553.A547M6 1985   813'.54   84-23904
ISBN 0-570-03970-3

---

1 2 3 4 5 6 7 8 9 10 MAL 94 93 92 91 90 89 88 87 86 85

The Lord said to [Abram]: "Know for certain that your descendants will be strangers in a country not their own, and they will be enslaved and mistreated four hundred years."

Genesis 15:13

Contents

Introduction

Mizraim!

The Hebrews called the place of their captivity "Mizraim." Spoken with a strong "z-z-z" sound, it hinted of the hiss of a snake.

The Egypt of the Pharaohs took its shape from the gently winding Nile, which nourished it. For hundreds of miles it was a narrow oasis between two deserts. Then where the river separated into seven branches toward the end of its northward flow it became a wide delta. Mizraim was long and slender—snakelike—with the delta as its head—or so it could be imagined.

Mizraim!

That was also the name of the father of the Egyptians. Mizraim was the grandson of Noah through the line of Ham.

The Hebrews, tracing their lineage back to Noah through the Semitic people who descended from Shem, guarded well against mixing the two lines. They were a separate people.

They took some pride in teaching succeeding generations of their children that Egypt had once been totally subjugated for 150 years to kindred Semites who came from Canaan and Syria—the formidable Hyksos.

They told them of Joseph, whom the Hyksos ruler freed from prison and elevated to second in command in Egypt. They told how the Hyksos had welcomed Jacob and his clan and given them the Wadi Tumilat area in Goshen as their haven from drought-ravaged Canaan.

The Hyksos rulers, called "Shepherd Kings," did not resemble their gentle-sounding title. Their armies surged over Egypt's border without provocation or warning. Swift-rolling chariots manned by expert archers, followed by waves of professional foot soldiers, overwhelmed the defenders of Mizraim.

The Hebrews knew the story well, even though all traces of the Hyksos era had been removed from Egypt's records. And this was the story:

Salitis, the Hyksos general, relentlessly drove his army past unfortified trading posts on Egypt's border. They thundered against hastily prepared defenses with such force and swiftness that key garrisons and cities fell without one major battle.

The invaders destroyed temples and public buildings— everything of value. Captives were shown no mercy. The Egyptian army was driven further and further south. Egypt floundered; the general of the army, Tutimaeus, surrendered.

Salitis set up temporary headquarters in Memphis. There was an enforced peace in the land; both Upper and Lower Egypt paid heavy tribute money to the Shepherd Kings.

The house of Jacob, favored under the long Hyksos rule, multiplied and prospered. They evidenced no great longing for Canaan.

The Hyksos prospered, too. They attempted to copy the sophisticated culture of Egypt, even giving their kings the title of Pharaoh. They had come to stay.

After nearly a century and a half they became less vigilant over the southern regions hundreds of miles from their new capital city, Avaris. And it was from the south, beginning at Thebes, that the revolt began.

The reigning Hyksos king, Apophis, could not stop the rebellion. Galleys headed north down the Nile carrying soldiers motivated by hate and revenge, determined to liberate their homeland.

One of the war's first victims was the insurgent leader, Sekenere. He was killed in hand-to-hand combat with a Hyksos who gashed his head five times with a long sword.

Sekenere's son, Ahmose, took up the fight with greater motivation.

The armies raged at each other. There were no quick victories. The strategically important Scharuhen was besieged for two years. Apophis's palace at Avaris was captured only after three heavy onslaughts, each with devastating losses on both sides.

When Avaris did fall, it was the signal of the end for the Semitic rulers. They retreated before the victorious army, whose ranks had been enhanced with mercenaries from Asia and Africa. These avengers, nourished by success, forged into their enemy's home territory and crushed the Hyksos empire—then went on to bring most of Canaan and Syria under their control as well.

Ahmose, son of Sekenere, became Ahmose I—Glorious Liberator of Egypt. He secured Egypt's borders from future surprise attacks by building a line of well-fortified outposts in a wide buffer area. The work was facilitated by tribute money and forced labor as his old enemies paid dearly.

Once semi-isolated, Egypt became a world power. It excelled in commerce and extended its influence by diplomacy and by the sword.

The descendants of Jacob stayed on in Egypt. There was no immediate indication that the change in political power should affect their way of life.

> Then a new king, who did not know about Joseph, came to power in Egypt. (Exodus 1:8)

Kohath, of the tribe of Levi, did not like the changes taking place in Goshen, but he stayed on—as did the other Hebrews.

The new Pharaoh, Seti the Great, was rebuilding Avaris and needed vast additional acreage for new arsenals, silos, marketplaces, administrative buildings and temples. Much of the land he needed was confiscated from the Hebrews, who were being edged into a smaller area in Goshen. For the first time in the nearly 400 years that they had been in Egypt, the Hebrews were being closely surrounded by a pagan culture. They felt the pressure of being considered a peculiar people, but they clung to the ways of their fathers.

Seti admired his renovated, enlarged Avaris so much that he made it the site of a grand celebration—the installation of his young son as coregent. The son's name was Rameses.

Gradually the pastoral life of most of the Hebrews vanished, and many of the people were forced into Pharaoh's labor crews. The times were difficult when Kohath's son, Amram, married Jochebed. Amram and Jochebed, descendants of Levi, followed the custom of marrying within their own tribe. They considered their future with apprehension. Because the Hebrews had been allied with the Hyksos regime they were suspect, and because they were suspect they were being subjected to increasing harassment.

Seti the Great died, leaving Rameses the sole occupant of the Egyptian throne—hereditary prince of the throne of Geb, the earth god.

One of Rameses' first priorities was to obliterate any last reminders of the Hyksos era. Their names were omitted from government records; battles that had been fought against them—even in the successful rebellion—were not celebrated. No one mentioned them—openly.

Early in Rameses' reign he waged wars with principalities in Canaan and Syria, but when he felt secure from invasion by predatory neighboring countries, he concentrated on expanding the building programs begun by his father.

Until then, the descendants of Jacob had been content to adjust to their smaller land allotments, had taken their turns with the building crews, and had tried to keep their children away from Egyptian influences as much as possible. But now their lives were drastically altered.

Part One

The Prince

1

They made their lives bitter with hard labor. . . . the Egyptians used them ruthlessly. *Exodus 1:14*

Amram and Gether talked about the Pharaoh almost as routinely as they mentioned the weather.

"Who does the man think he is? Another Seti?" Amram's voice carried more agitation than usual.

"He's no Seti. Seti was merely outrageous; Rameses is incredible!" Gether clenched his fists and struggled to control his voice. "I think the whole pantheon of Egyptian deities is driving him to his absurd passion to build, build, build."

"Uzal says we should be glad he has become occupied with erecting monuments to himself; at least he is not starting up any more wars. But I would as soon be in his army as work on endless labor details!"

"No! War wouldn't be any solution; you know that! Besides, we never would be called to fight in Pharaoh's army. They say he already loses sleep, worrying about our getting access to arms or an opportunity to join with his enemies— to send the Egyptians south for another hundred years or so."

"Sounds like a good idea!"

"Quiet! Talk like that is dangerous—for the one who speaks and for the one who listens!" Gether glanced around to see if anyone had heard. He lowered his voice and forced a smile that was calculated to calm Amram. "We don't have things too hard. We only take our turn with all the other peasants who work in the royal labor force."

"Royal labor force? Slavery! It's *slavery!*"

"No, my friend, not slavery. There are limits on the number of weeks we must work. It's not a constant way of life, and it won't be—if hotheads like you don't get us into trouble by agitating."

"I'm not an agitator. I just see things as they are, and I'm not afraid to say it out."

"Does a realist have to be so noisy?"

"Only if it's necessary in order to get other people to listen!"

Their conversations were typical of the feelings among the Hebrews. Some were apprehensive, wondering if they should attempt revolt before it was too late. Some believed it was better to live with their present situation and keep things peaceful, hoping their lot didn't become worse.

Rameses, delighted with the glitter of burgeoning Avaris, designated it his capital city. He renamed it Rameses and ordered a grand temple to be built in it, dedicated to himself. He would work with the architects personally on the details of the temple. It would be built on a large scale and would be flanked by two great statues of himself, each 40 feet high.

Although things were going well for Rameses, he was increasingly haunted by fears of insurrection—of conspiracy between his beleaguered subjects and his abundant enemies. His father had talked with him, confidentially, of the cataclysm caused by the Hyksos. His fears evolved into an obsessive mind-set, linking the Israelites to that terrible time. They became a continuous reminder of the officially ignored Hyksos occupation force—of the 150 years of Egyptian humiliation when they lived as serfs in their own land.

He regarded it as a myth that one of the Hebrews had actually saved Egypt from famine and secured for the nation, even though it was under Hyksos rule, a prestigious worldwide renown. He was convinced only that they must have collaborated with the invaders and would do it again.

And so Rameses sought to make sure they would not have that opportunity. He devised a simple solution. The Hebrews would no longer work on his projects on a rotation basis; they would be a permanent work force. There would be no countenancing of the slightest defiance; they would be good slaves—or they would die.

By official decree of the Pharaoh, one nation was reduced to slavery; another nation was debased by implementing it.

When a sweating slave stood to ease his aching muscles or tired back, an overseer was within his authority to snap, "The rod is in my hand! Don't be idle!"

The slave could choose the sting of the snakelike whip or stoop immediately to his work so as not to be guilty of rebellion—against Mizraim!

With a vast work force secured, Pharaoh's next order of business was to build a store city similar to Rameses in the southern part of Goshen. The new city was named Pithom, and it was to occupy part of the valley between the Nile and Lake Timsah. It would be as fine as the city of Rameses and would be dedicated to the sun god Atum.

Rameses in the north and Pithom in the south of Goshen—the area became densely populated, and precious acres were consumed by the extravagant public buildings, temples and new housing. The descendants of Jacob were gradually crowded into a smaller and smaller space.

Amram was sent to Pithom and assigned to the higher-risk work of carrying heavy limestone facing up steep ramps to scaffoldings where masons, chained together, worked on the new city's elaborate landmarks. Like other Hebrews, he was constantly aware of his demeaning status as a slave and, just as others did, he suffered the systematic berating of overseers and occasionally was lashed. But Amram was never robbed of his basic self-esteem, and he took pride in knowing that he carried those stone blocks to heights that made others dizzy. Because of his expertise he felt the whip less often than those with lesser skills did. Construction chiefs with a quota of work to get done on time didn't want to incapacitate a man who was proficient at a dangerous job.

He had escaped the drudgery of collecting sand and clay from the riverbank and carrying it in baskets to the brick-yards. He didn't have to mix clay with sand, water and chopped straw and then tread that mixture in vats with his bare feet day after day after day. He escaped the tedious task of putting the clay mixture into molds and removing the bricks one by one after they were sunbaked. He didn't have to help dig new channels for the Nile or work in the dark limestone quarries at Ma'sarah. Workers in all these menial jobs could be replaced easily, so they were driven hard, underfed, ill clad, deprived of sanitary conditions, and whipped at the slightest provocation. Their death rate was high.

Slaves with the highest mortality rate of all were those who had to move, inch by inch, the gigantic masses of stone block on wooden rollers from barges to the places where they would be used in building Pharaoh's latest fancy. The stone movers often fell from the brutal strain. If they couldn't get back on their feet, they were left by the roadside to die or to be executed as deserters.

When they could manage it, friends and relatives met in some brave person's home to complain about their problems and to encourage each other. Their best encouragement came from the prophecy given to their father Abraham; it concerned their long stay in an alien land. There were few Hebrews who could not recite it:

> Know for certain that your descendants will be strangers in a country not their own, and they will be enslaved and mistreated four hundred years. But I will punish the nation they serve as slaves, and afterward they will come out with great possessions. . . . In the fourth generation your descendants will come back here.

Those ancient words gave great hope to the men and women of Amram and Jochebed's time, for the 400 years were nearly ended!

Meanwhile, if Amram had to be a slave, he was glad he could climb high!

2

Relent, O Lord! How long will it be?
Have compassion on your servants.

Psalm 90:13

Rameses and Pithom became well-established cities, and the work on the fortress at Pithom was finally almost finished. The fortress had been enlarged and made more ornate in the course of its long completion.

Amram's overseers had noticed that his agility in climbing up the ramps had deteriorated, and for the last 24 months he had been doing less physically demanding work; he had been assigned to a stone-carving crew. He quickly evidenced a talent for handling chisel and hammer and again had work in which he could take pride. He was thankful for the change in occupation because he had become less confident about his ability to continue to handle the stone facings at great heights—the years were taking a heavy toll.

A crippling fall would have been all the more disastrous because he was the father of a beautiful daughter and a fine son—Miriam and Aaron. They, and their mother, were his chief joy. But at times his beloved family was also the reason for his bitterest sorrow—like the time Aaron asked, "What work will I be trained to do, Father?"

"What would you like to do?" Amram's tone was wistful; his words were meaningless.

Aaron, dreaming his seven-year-old's dreams, answered, "I'd like to carry stone to the top of the highest thing in Egypt. Then I'd like to carve on stone. I want to be just like you."

It was a moment for a father to treasure, and he patted Aaron's shoulder. Then fury flooded his mind: No! *No!* Not like me! *Not a slave!*

A lifetime effort at self-control kept him from shouting his feelings. He accepted the accolade his son had given him. "Aaron, every father hopes his son can do better than whatever he, or anyone else, ever has done before. So . . . if you carve on stone, may it be for Mizraim's finest monument, and if you climb with stone facings or bricks, may it be to the highest scaffolding in the land!"

Aaron's face flushed with pride. He saw himself grown up, defying death high above the heads of other slaves. Carving monuments could wait.

Jochebed and Miriam were sitting just outside the door, weaving straw mats by the last light of early evening; they heard the conversation of Amram and Aaron. Miriam tossed her head and tilted her chin. Her dark eyes closed as if to keep from seeing what she was about to describe. Her voice was eloquent because of its very lack of emotion.

"I know what I'll do when I'm older . . . marry a man of the tribe of Levi and have children. There will not be enough to feed them, not enough room to make them comfortable. And I'll weave straw mats and cook and clean and wash clothes for almost more hours than there are in a day."

Miriam's cynical wisdom made her seem older than her 12 years. Robbed of childhood's joy and freedom, apprehensive of her future, she looked now at her mother with eyes that begged: Tell me I'm wrong. Tell me there's to be more than this!

Jochebed groped for words to help her daughter face life as it must be lived. "Would you rather work in fields . . . or carry water to brickmakers or to the men who drag the heavy stone blocks? Women who don't have children to care for find themselves ordered to do many different kinds of work."

She had tried to give her daughter the bleak alternatives available as gently as possible, but Miriam's rage increased, and her voice showed it. "You know I've heard what the women say: 'Provide slaves for the future, or join the work force yourself.' Well . . . I won't! I won't give Mizraim any of my children as slaves, and I won't be one either!"

Jochebed admired her daughter's spirit but looked around uneasily to see if anyone other than family might have heard her tirade. She turned back to Miriam and tried again to soothe away some of her frustration. "Women have felt as you do before and have said what you have said . . . but things don't change because of helpless resolves.

"Miriam, my sweet one, it's good to have children. I count you and Aaron as blessings from the Lord God. And to have a husband who cares for you and respects you . . . that's good, too."

Miriam stood up quickly, pitching her unfinished mat as far from her as she could. "Our household is more fortunate than too many others! My father hasn't been worked to death or beaten into disability . . . yet. But I won't be part of Mizraim. I *will not* have a baby who must grow up in slavery. And I *will not be a slave!* If the only other choice is death . . . then I will die!"

A torrent of words of advice, reprimand, encouragement—and frustration—came into Jochebed's mind. She didn't know which words to choose—so she said nothing.

The eyes of mother and daughter met, and each discerned the other's helplessness to make things right—or even to understand fully.

The tense quiet between them became oppressive, and Jochebed ended it by speaking her daughter's name with all the love and compassion she could put into one word: "Miriam . . ."

The girl looked toward her mother with all the defiance she wanted to hurl at her miserable world—to squelch anything Jochebed might have wanted to say. Then she stomped over to the discarded mat, kicked it further away, and turned and went into the house.

Jochebed watched as Miriam stalked away. She remembered herself at Miriam's age—just as indignant, just as certain that personal defiance against Mizraim was possible.

She had come to terms with her lot long ago. She accepted herself and her circumstances and learned to make the best of both. She knew Miriam would do that, too, although for now she must have a few wild dreams.

Jochebed was strong—physically, emotionally and intellectually—but she was vulnerable to depression when she thought of her son and daughter as slaves. The best she could do for them was teach them to face life honestly and to see good even in hard situations—when that was possible. She allowed them their own strengths and weaknesses without trying to conform them to her own.

And when she thought of the winding down of the "four hundred years" and remembered the certainty of the Lord God's promises to Abraham, Isaac and Jacob, she could hope Miriam's determined stand against Mizraim would hold.

The words sometimes almost sang themselves into her mind: "In the fourth generation your descendants will come back here." Levi, Kohath, Amram, and Aaron—there had been four generations since the patriarch Israel had brought his family as strangers to Mizraim. She believed that Aaron and Miriam would see Canaan—beautiful, beloved, and much-longed-for Canaan.

Pharaoh had turned most of Egypt into a building site. He commissioned more, larger and grander things than any previous Pharaoh. Still, he was never satisfied. As ornate structures, great cities and long highways came into being at his direction, he was only frustrated, perplexed and enraged that more could not be accomplished. The name of Rameses the Great must eclipse that of any other Pharaoh. He never was certain he had done enough to ensure that. Then, in what he considered an astounding burst of brilliance, he devised a plan: Elite stone workers would carve the monogram of Rameses the Great on previously erected temples, obelisks, pylons, colonnades and sanctuaries of his choosing—branding them as his own!

Amram had been assigned to this group. Their work often took them away from home for long periods of time.

In the darkness of late evening Amram sat in his doorway. He gave the appearance of being drowsy, but it was only a ruse to keep from talking—to keep delaying what he must tell his wife. He turned to watch her busily setting out the straw for the next day's weaving and humming softly as she did it. He sighed and shrugged his shoulders. He might as well get it over with since she had to know.

"Jochebed . . . tomorrow I leave again. The stone carvers are to work on something of great concern to Pharaoh. We will go south . . . to Memphis or maybe even Thebes or Luxor."

Jochebed made a little gasp, covered her lips quickly with her hand, and asked the question that was on Amram's mind, too: "Do you think you will be home by the time . . . ?"

"By the time our third child is born? Yes. Even if I have to run away!"

"Amram, don't talk foolishness. Don't put thoughts of your being a hunted slave in my mind." She knelt beside him and welcomed the warmth of his embrace—until he spoke to her. "No need to worry; that was only idle talk."

She drew herself free from his arms; she still was troubled. She thought of Miriam's resentment, which had continued to grow. "Don't dismiss it as 'idle talk.' Even if the Egyptians don't hear you, our children do. Miriam is her father's daughter; she shares your longing for freedom *and* your frequent need to make it vocal. She parrots her philosophy to everyone around, and I believe she would say it to Pharaoh himself: 'I won't bear or be a slave.' "

Amram's face registered more pride than dismay. "Good! She has listened to her father, and she has remembered your own teachings, too."

"My teachings? I never taught disobedience . . . rebellion!"

"But you have taught our children about Abraham and the covenant promise . . . including the prophesied four hundred years of exile. You've told Miriam and Aaron this number of years will soon have passed. Have you not given them reason to be restless with our present situation?"

"I never meant to make them restless. I've tried to teach that waiting on the Lord God—even when waiting seems a waste of precious time—is evidence of faith.

"I've taught our children what we've been taught by our elders: that the Lord God spoke to Abraham, to Isaac and to Jacob when He was ready to reveal steps in His plan . . . and that He will speak to the one He chooses as His next servant.

"It's His own Word to His people, written long ago and guarded by every generation. . . . which tells us that the time for our deliverance must be soon. But this teaching should bring peace, not restlessness!"

Jochebed had spoken with assurance, but her eyes pleaded for her husband's understanding. She took very seriously the instruction of their children.

Amram smiled approval. "I'm having difficulty finding words acceptable to you. You didn't like 'idle talk' and you don't like 'restless.'

"Let's not waste any more moments of this night in speaking about shades of meanings of words. You are the best teacher our children could have; I leave them in your care when I'm gone with no worries about their safety or instruction. They are blessed to have such a mother, and I am blessed to have such a wife."

The next morning, before daybreak, a whip-carrying o-verseer banged on the door of Amram's house. He was rounding up the men whose privilege it was to serve Rameses the Great.

3

Pharaoh gave this order to all his people: "Every boy that is born you must throw into the river, but let every girl live."

Exodus 1:22

By the time Jochebed and her children had eaten breakfast, Amram was with his crew on a barge headed south on the Nile. His family ate in silence, each preoccupied with private thoughts.

Miriam considered her father's forced move at a time when a baby was soon due as further proof that she must defy, however possible, the atrocity of slavery.

Aaron thought that since he was to be the man of the house for a while, he would assume that role immediately. He cleared his throat and asked for a second helping of curds and milk.

Jochebed absentmindedly gave it to him while Miriam looked on in astonishment. Only Father got second helpings!

As she worked on the straw mats that morning, Jochebed still wondered if Amram would come home again in time for the birth of their newest child—or if he might ever come home at all; so many "accidents" happened to slaves.

Then for a while she allowed herself to wonder if their new little one might just possibly live to become more than a slave.

Before that day was over she had reason to fear that her baby might not live at all—even to be a slave!

At midmorning uniformed messengers moved through the streets of Pithom, proclaiming Pharaoh's latest edict. At first the women heard the news with stunned disbelief; then as their shock wore away they became hysterical.

By late afternoon the neighborhood women were congregating at the well, their usual meeting place. They came to talk with each other of the unbelievable, to try to find a measure of consolation by sharing their desperation and, failing that, to weep together.

They had done this on a lesser scale before—to vent their feelings about forced labor laws, new deprivations of needed rations, dispersion of families. But those issues were dwarfed by this new law being inflicted on them. On this day they were almost incoherent as they agonized over the monstrous ultimatum: Their infant sons were to be killed at the moment of birth!

Jochebed stood a little apart from the other women. She looked down at her hands, fingers interlaced and resting on her abdomen, which was large with a child who might be as good as dead.

She glanced back toward the women, hoping Pharaoh's messengers wouldn't come back with whips to break up the pathetic crowd. Apparently they would leave the women alone for a while; perhaps they enjoyed watching this dramatic but ineffectual reaction.

Ordinarily she would have been in the midst of the clamoring women, taking the lead. But just then she could not find words to fit the fierce emotions ravaging her mind, making her ill. She had started to walk back to her home when she heard someone raise an authoritative voice. She turned back to see Shiphrah with her right arm raised high, demanding quiet.

Everyone knew Shiphrah. She was one of the two designated women responsible for training and supervising more than 500 midwives in Goshen. She was trusted by both Egyptians and Hebrews as a woman of competence and caring.

Shiphrah spoke now without emotion. Jochebed sensed that if the midwife had allowed any feeling to creep into her voice she would choke on her words.

"My co-worker, Puah, and I are sent this day to confirm what was told to you by Pharaoh's messengers. She and I have been talking to women in different parts of Goshen since early morning to tell what our orders are from this moment on.

"Listen. I will say this just once. There will be nothing new in my message, nothing you don't already know from the royal decree. But Pharaoh believes that by hearing it from Puah or me you women will grasp more fully his law concerning male Hebrew babies.

"Puah and I were called to the palace for a meeting with Pharaoh. He told us that when midwives help Hebrew women in childbirth and observe that a boy has been born, he is to be killed. The manner of death is left up to us.

"Girl babies will be allowed to live."

Shiphrah finished her toneless speech. Now as she looked at the women standing in front of her, tears filled her eyes—communicating a compassion her voice had lacked.

It was then Jochebed managed to speak out. She stood alone, still off to the side of the group, so it was easy to call to Shiphrah, who was using the cover of the well as a platform.

"Shiphrah! Do you fear Pharaoh more than you fear the Lord God?"

The midwife had spent many years among the Hebrew women and had heard of the power of their God who was called by magnificent names such as Elohim, El Shaddai, El Elyon. Now, challenged by Jochebed's words, she felt for the first time a personal awe of Him. Could she risk the wrath of such a one?

Shiphrah's eyes met Jochebed's, then glanced toward the chariot where her driver and armed honor guard waited.

Jochebed's clear question rang out again: "Do you fear Pharaoh more than the Lord God?"

Shiphrah turned so the Egyptians couldn't see her face. Trusting fervently in the Hebrew women's notable talent for discernment she called for their attention again. Then with a knowing smile that was meant to convey understanding and even some hope of assistance, she said with deliberate emphasis, "I have come to you with the message Pharaoh told me to bring. As his representative I will not answer the question about fearing a god he does not recognize."

The listening Egyptians were satisfied that she was loyal to Pharaoh. The Hebrew women thanked the Lord God for both the sympathy and the fragile hope Shiphrah subtly communicated to them.

During the next month, as far as Jochebed knew, not one male child was murdered. She marveled at the midwives' courage and wondered how long they could continue to defy Rameses.

The women talked often of Shiphrah and Puah and their corps of workers when they went to the well for their daily supply of water. They had shaken off much of their earlier fear.

"Let Pharaoh make rules, and let the midwives break them."

"They are brave women."

"Do you suppose they ever are afraid of what might happen to them because of their helping us?"

"Rameses is busy looking after his building projects. He has already forgotten about the baby boys of the Hebrew families."

There was a feeling of childlike joy at being part of a revolution against tyranny.

But Rameses had not forgotten. He had merely been away on an inspection trip in the south. On returning to his palace he learned that his edict for infanticide had not been carried out. He was furious.

Soldiers were dispatched to escort Shiphrah and Puah to the throne room. Aides were instructed to bring them in to him the moment they arrived. While he waited, his anger increased.

Shiphrah and Puah walked into the throne room with an outward serenity that gave no hint of their terror. Shiphrah was finding it difficult to be more in awe of an unseen God than of this menacing man who regarded slavery, torture and murder as legitimate punishments. She silently said the names she knew for the God of the Hebrews as she walked to the throne and bowed: Elohim. El Shaddai. El Elyon. El Olam.

Rameses jumped to his feet. His imperious voice filled the room as he thundered out at the women. "Why? Why have you let boy babies of the slave people live?"

He expected a sentimental plea for the innocents. He expected the women to beg for mercy for themselves. He shouted again, "Speak—*now!*"

In her most official tone Shiphrah offered an explanation. "The Hebrew women are not like the Egyptian women. They are vigorous and give birth before the midwives arrive."

Puah was aghast at her companion's contrived defense. She tried not to show her surprise but felt her face suddenly warmed by new fear.

Pharaoh was livid at Shiphrah's insolence! She insulted his intelligence. He stood in silent rage, pondering a suitable fate for these two who dared to disobey him and then embarrass him in front of his ministers. After reasoning briefly with himself, he decided he would not allow martyrdom or even arrest to focus attention on them and their cause. He would sentence them to obscurity.

He motioned for his scribe to come to him. "Write! Shiphrah and Puah are no longer qualified to supervise the midwives in Goshen, nor shall they themselves be allowed to assist at any births. I will announce their successors after reviewing likely candidates.

"Write! To all my subjects: Every Hebrew boy that is born you must throw into the river, but . . ." He paused for dramatic effect, then with a grand sweep of his right arm he made a bizarre attempt at graciousness. "But . . . let every girl live."

Pharaoh swept from the throne room, followed by his ministers. He would show everyone that he decreed who lived—or died—in Egypt!

4

By faith Moses' parents hid him for three months after he was born, because they saw he was no ordinary child, and they were not afraid of the king's edict.   *Hebrews 11:23*

N o records were kept of how many babies were destroyed. It's just as well. Tragedy can't be tabulated; terror can't be summed up in columns; feelings lose much of their acute pain when they are translated into words and numbers.

Hebrew families attempted to fight back. They organized groups to keep continuous lookout for approaching search squads. When the watchers whistled an alarm, it was relayed again and again; a deafening din started up throughout the neighborhood. Children, acting as decoys, imitated crying babies and lured the hunters off the track. There was frantic banging of spoons on pans and musical instruments were played—anything to drown out infant wails and confuse the searchers!

While this went on, mothers snatched up tiny sons, wrapped them in sheets and put them into large baskets covered loosely with reeds or tucked them into boxes and placed them on shelves inside the chimney. If there was time, the box could be taken outside, put in a trench and covered loosely with leaves. A chronic crybaby would get a sip of wine to make him sleep; a suddenly fretful one would get a taste of sweet fruit juice to placate him.

The Hebrew women no longer had the services of midwives, so they helped each other. Now not only the mother risked her life in childbirth, but the women who assisted her did also.

The watchers, often slaves who never got enough rest or sleep even in ordinary times, were pushed to new extremes of endurance.

Each person's newborn son became everyone's newborn son. The male infants were hidden, protected and defended until they were wrenched from their families, who tried never to look at the crocodile-infested Nile again.

Against this background, Amram and Jochebed's third child was born.

Amram's group returned to Goshen after more than two months in Thebes. The men were released to go their separate ways without being told of the infanticide that had begun while they were away, but before he reached his house, Amram learned of it. A neighbor, Eli, saw him first and ran down the street to meet him and tell him what had happened. Amram's mind would not accept it. Oppressing adults was one thing, but killing children—infants!

Amram hurried toward his house. Eli kept up with him, still trying to convince him of the tragedy that had come on the people. Amram's response to every word of Eli's was *"No!"*

Gether, who lived next door to Amram, heard the two men talking but didn't look up until they stopped by his doorway. He really didn't know how long he had been sitting there.

"Gether, what do you know about all this . . . this decree Eli is talking about?"

Gether looked for a long time at the disbelief in Amram's face. Then this strong man whose emotion was overspent rose slowly and walked over to greet his friend. His words came with difficulty.

"Shalom, my friend. It is good that you are home. Your wife will need you."

"Gether, what is Eli talking about? I don't understand."

"What he told you is true." Gether placed his large, calloused hands on Amram's shoulders and softly continued, "My wife can no longer say a word; she only cries. Our son lived four days."

Amram embraced his friend. Sympathy for Hannah and Gether and their son was spontaneous, then it competed with apprehension about his own child, soon to be born. In another instant both sympathy and fear gave way to searing, irrational thoughts of revenge. In his mind he raced back to the place he had just worked to obliterate with his own hands the inscriptions of Rameses' name that he had helped carve on monuments and buildings! Then he imagined finding Rameses and flinging him into the Nile. Such fantasies were senseless except to work off fragments of the savage emotions that made this weary slave forget he was tired.

"I will come back to talk with you more, Gether. I must go to Jochebed now."

"Yes. I will go in to Hannah also . . . to try to get her to eat some broth. . . . Jochebed brought some to her."

The friends parted before either could see the other's tears.

Amram went quickly to his own door and through it to Jochebed. Their love for each other and their joy to be together again was communicated in a wordless moment. It wasn't the time for conversation. Between sobs Jochebed began to say what she had been thinking ever since her labor pains had begun several hours earlier.

"Amram, I want our child to be a girl. In spite of the way things are . . . I want my child . . . to know life! So . . . I . . . want this baby . . . to be another daughter. I do. Oh! I do!"

Amram took her in his arms, offering solace but refraining from speaking. He thought it best not to share with her just then his abiding belief that this would be a son—not just an ordinary one but one to be used in a special way by the Lord God. He hadn't told anyone of his conviction for fear of ridicule. The thought was too high, too wondrous for him to risk its being derided or considered merely the wishful imagining of a father. This strong impression had come to him time after time as he prayed for enslaved Israel. He soon would know if the baby was a boy, and if so, in a few years he would know if what he now believed would be confirmed.

In the next hours Amram's cottage was filled with hope and fear, travail and joy; the atmosphere was pervaded with prayers that the one about to be born would be granted a life rich in meaning, full of years.

The baby was a boy—healthy, squirming, crying—certainly the most handsome baby in the world! Amram felt vindicated already in his daring hope for this child. Jochebed wouldn't have traded him for any infant girl in Goshen. Aaron had a special reason to help in the noisemaking that had become almost a game—a dangerous but important game. Miriam decided she wanted to be a watcher.

The baby grew; he usually was contented and quiet. The family adjusted to their new tensions and learned their protective roles well, performing them with skill and instant innovations. Aaron believed his bellowing cries were heard further than any other boy's in his section of town. He was sure he could lead all Egyptian scouts away from his helpless brother.

Too often, the programmed noise in the settlement was pierced by shrieks of horror. Each time a baby was found and taken away, a chilling, knifelike pain pierced the heart of every mother and father, terrorized every brother and sister.

Frequently a few men congregated in Uzal's cottage. At other times their conversation would have been of daily happenings, the weather, general news that anyone happened to hear. But now their talk centered on the present crisis and the terrifying result if it continued much longer.

Gether, still shattered from his recent experience, spoke with finality. "Our people should stop having children. I wish we had not had a son four weeks ago. We will have no more."

His host was shocked. "But with no children for a new generation, our people will cease to exist!"

Ophir thought that sounded like blasphemy and said so. "Our Lord God promised that the descendants of Abraham will endure through all time. His word is true. We can't become extinct."

Gether would not be dissuaded from his pessimism. "Why can't we? It's begun to happen."

Amram added his own philosophy. "Our people are stifled and sodden. Where are the rebels? Where are the hopeful ones?"

Gether looked at Amram disdainfully. "Rebels would be lunatics. To be hopeful now would be madness."

Uzal seemed not to have heard his guests' chatter. His expression hadn't changed since he mentioned the possibility of the seed of Abraham ceasing to exist. Now, enlarging on that, he spoke in a soft voice, strained and weakened by age and unending hard labor. "Pharaoh couldn't destroy us by demoralizing us in slavery or by inflicting his many cruelties. But now he will win . . . through our children . . . through our dead children!" He had spoken slowly, regretting every word he said, but feeling he must tell how things seemed to him.

The conversation was having a dismal effect on Ophir, who only moments before had tried to find reason to think the Lord God would intervene. "And just when we thought it was about time for a deliverer to come . . ."

Amram had to respond! He wanted to wait for a while—to make certain—but now he must say it. His belief in the potential of his child increased with each day. "Who knows but that the deliverer is already among us? As Ophir said a while ago, 'Our God *is* faithful.' He *will* keep His covenant."

Gether lashed out a challenge, "If the deliverer is among us, why doesn't he make himself known?

"He . . . may be . . . too young."

Gether jumped up from his bench in exasperation. "So that's it! You've begun to think your own son is to be our great leader! Tell us, Amram, is this your idea or did the Lord God tell you? Say it right!"

"I haven't heard Him speak, if that's what you mean."

"Then how could you even think such a thing? Even if I believed you, even if it were true . . . we will be dead by the time your baby is old enough to be of any help to us!"

Amram knew it was useless to argue; there was skepticism in the faces of the other men. He felt sorry for them; they looked like men without hope. As for him—he believed what he believed.

The new baby was two and a half months old. Soldiers had come to the house twice that week without finding him, but they had come back for the third try. Jochebed responded to the warning whistle, and her son was hidden away before the soldiers pushed open the door. They stomped in, looked around, ransacked the three rooms, then left to go to the next place on their list.

Jochebed sighed with relief; then the crisis developed. One of the soldiers came back in, looking suspicious and listening intently. He scanned the emptied out clothesbaskets and reexamined their contents that were still scattered all over the room. He kicked the bedding that lay in a pile on the floor.

Jochebed's heart pounded so hard she thought the searcher would hear it. He didn't. The baby had been quiet for so long, she was certain he would cry soon. He did.

As a muffled whimper came from the chimney where a cushioned box rested on a shelf, Jochebed began to cough, loudly! She kept on coughing until the soldier was annoyed.

"Can't you stop that coughing, woman?"

"No." She coughed again to prove it. Her throat was getting irritated by the coughing and that made it easier to carry on the bluff. "And it's contagious, very contagious. You better hurry out of here!"

She thought the corners of his mouth turned up a bit, as though he might smile. Her heart, which had been beating so hard up until then, now seemed to stand still.

But Pharaoh's soldier simply said, "You may be right. I don't want to catch that cough."

He hurried from the house without seeing the delight that transformed Jochebed's face, without hearing another whimper from the chimney shelf and a mother's soothing response.

Jochebed told Amram the incredible story when he came home that evening. He listened with delight but without surprise. "Do you think he heard our baby cry?"

"Yes."

"Do you think he left so quickly because he was afraid of your cough?"

"No."

"Well . . . do you suppose Rameses' soldiers have gone softhearted?"

"No."

"Then how do you explain what happened? Why is our son not dead in the waters of the Nile?"

"I can't explain it . . . only . . . well . . ." She wouldn't say what she thought, for it would sound presumptuous; she truly believed their son had been spared miraculously.

Amram reached to take her hand. "I've dreamed of his future, and the dream is a large one."

"Amram, I believe the Lord God has given us each the same dream."

And so without putting it into words, they understood each other, and they felt their faith in the destiny of their son—and of their people—was confirmed.

The baby was three months old. Jochebed and Amram were convinced that the Lord God was protecting their son. They still were careful about letting outsiders know of his existence, and they still followed the safety procedures set up for the good of all the babies—but they did it in trust, not in fear.

——————————————————————5

When she could hide him no longer, she got a papyrus basket
for him and coated it with tar and pitch. Then she placed the
child in it and put it among the reeds along the bank of the
Nile.   *Exodus 2:3*

Jochebed cradled her little son on her lap. She
let his tiny hand grasp her finger, gently rocked him, and
treasured the peaceful moments. There had been many
times like this in the last two weeks.

She was amazed at how rested she felt. The apprehension
she had been under the weeks before that afternoon of her
"coughing spell" had taken more strength than she had realized. She still worked long hours each day caring for her
baby; she still rushed to hide him when the search squads
came; she still tended to the needs of all her family and
managed to weave a few mats. But now it was done without
anxiety, and that made a refreshing difference.

She often thought of Shiphrah and Puah. The talk at the
well was that they no longer were allowed to supervise the
midwives and couldn't personally attend either Hebrew or
Egyptian women. Then just recently Yinatan had heard at
the marketplace that neither of the former midwives had
been punished yet, that they were living comfortably with
their families. Yoahaz thought it was possible that Pharaoh
was still deciding what to do with them—and that it would
be very, very bad if it took him all this time to plan it.

Jochebed gently moved her baby to her other arm, cud-
dling him closer. She believed that those two wonderful
women had not been harmed because the Lord God was

protecting and rewarding them for their courageous help to
His people.

Rays of sunlight were slanting through the small latticed
window by the door. The brief time for resting, thinking,
and just being a "new mother" again had ended. There was
much to do.

Her son was sleeping. She still laid him in the cushioned
box that could be hidden on a shelf or in a garden trench at
a moment's notice.

She began to prepare supper. She was a good cook and
enjoyed fixing their simple meals from vegetables and fruit
that their garden supplied. Tonight she had planned an extra
surprise for after dinner. For her children there would be
pomegranates and for her and Amram a little sweet wine
from Kenherne. She had traded many straw mats for these
treats.

Amram was late. Miriam and Aaron were hungry, so she
let them eat. She planned to wait to eat with Amram.

The children finished eating—pomegranates and all—
then went to a neighbor's house to play a circle game of
"going around four times" before it got dark.

The baby was still sleeping. The house was quiet except
for the melody Jochebed hummed.

She caught herself looking out into the street every few
minutes. She became conscious of a growing uneasiness and
was impatient with herself, for she thought she had overcome being anxious. But why was he this late? A cooking
fire still smoldered on the brazier; it soon would go out.

At dusk she went outside to call Miriam and Aaron to
come home. She thought she saw her husband walking
slowly down the street, but at second glance she recognized
Ophir. She walked out to meet him.

She had never seen him look more serious; his eyes
would not meet hers.

"I've walked a long way, and I'm thirsty. May we go
back to your house so you can give me some water?"

"Yes, of course, Ophir. It is a warm evening."

"It is."

That was all they said until they had gone back to the house. Then before she could bring the water to him, he asked her to sit down. She obeyed his gentle voice as though she were hypnotized.

"You know we've been working on the new fortress."

"Yes."

"The work has gone well; it's almost finished. Amram's work is the finest he has ever done."

Jochebed wondered why Amram's best work on a nearly finished project could be the reason for Ophir's somber attitude—and her husband's late homecoming—and her own growing dread. She waited for Ophir to continue, but when he didn't, she said, "I know Amram is pleased with his work. He likes to tell us about the elaborate facade of the fortress. He says it's fit for a palace. Amram keeps saying that . . ."

"Yes!" Ophir interrupted. He had delayed telling her long enough; it must be done. "Yes, it's almost like a palace . . . almost as grand as a temple. Amram has never worked on a temple before, but there is to be a grand one built at Abu Simbel in Nubia. It's to be the finest in the world. They tell us the face of it will be 90 feet wide, carved out of the limestone hill—with the temple itself cut back into the cliff. It will be built fronting the river, and there will be four statues of Rameses, each more than 60 feet high, flanking it. Only expert craftsmen are assigned to it."

Now it was Jochebed's turn to interrupt. She grasped for another moment before hearing what she knew he would say. "I'd rather Amram would just work on fortresses all his life, if they are in Pithom or close by. I know Amram always has to do the most . . . be the best; but he wouldn't want to work in Nubia even if his overseer did think he was good enough to work there. He would . . ."

"Jochebed, you are right. He would rather work in Pithom or Rameses . . . but even talented slaves are . . . slaves. He had no choice. He was not even given time to come home to tell you. He is on a barge with others on the way to Abu Simbel."

"How long will he be gone?"

"It will be a life work."

"I'll take the children and go where he is. I'll . . ."

"No. Hebrews can't leave Goshen except with a labor crew. You know that."

Her shoulders sagged, and as she gradually bent forward, burying her face in her hands, the wrenching, silent sobs began.

Ophir would have preferred that she scream or cry out. The quiet was eerie, unnerving to him. He felt he should say something. He wished he had brought his wife along; Lael would have been able to comfort her. He reached out to touch her head in a token of sympathy, but she drew back, straightened her shoulders again and began to dab at her eyes and nose with the back of her hand.

Her voice was almost under control when she finally responded to Ophir's reminder of the limited options Mizraim gave to slaves.

"Yes, I know. I can't go with him. It was just my . . . heart speaking."

She stood up to let him know he was free to leave her house of sorrow. Her tears welled again as she thought of Ophir going home to his wife and children, where supper would be waiting. She spoke again and her voice was low, but as the words came, they brought with them a certain strength. "Thank you, my friend, for coming; it was hard for you to tell me.

"Now, will you find Miriam and Aaron. . . . They should be playing at the home of Mehidan. Tell them it's late and they should come home.

"I won't tell them about their father until morning. By then I will find a way to say it . . . somehow."

"Do you want Lael to come to stay with you tonight?"

"No . . . but thank you. I need quiet time . . . to think . . . to plan.

"Just . . . tell my children . . . to hurry home."

Jochebed watched the grey light of dawn come through the high window beside the door. She had not slept all night, merely waited for the morning that would begin not just a new day but a new phase of her life.

She felt as though there had been a death—as though Amram suddenly existed no more. And yet—somewhere—he watched the same sunrise she did and longed for her as much as she did for him. She wondered how the actual death of a mate could be more difficult than this!

She had told Ophir she wanted to spend the first hours without her husband making plans for herself and her children. How little she had understood how difficult it would be. With her mind reeling in confusion, planning was impossible.

Even a way to explain it to Miriam and Aaron escaped her. She had practiced a dozen ways, and none of them suited her.

She moved softly to look at her sleeping children—first the baby in the little box bed, then the other two. How would she care for them? Could relatives help? Would Miriam and Aaron soon be called to join Pharaoh's work force? She felt a crescendo of fear and rebellion and suffocating sorrow before the tears came again—before she could bring herself to pray for the peace and strength she would need to meet her new responsibilities.

She decided to use Ophir's words to tell Miriam and Aaron of Amram's forced move. She could think of no way more comforting than his. And so after breakfast she began. "Children, do you know the great fortress your father has been working on . . . the grand one that looks almost like a palace or a temple? Well . . ."

When her story was told and initial tears were shed, she put her arms around her son and daughter, assuring them they would stay together and keep their baby safe.

As if he heard himself being discussed, the son for whom Amram held such high hopes cried out for attention. It was a welcome excuse to end an emotionally charged conversation.

"We'll talk more later. I must feed the baby now; it's past his nursing time."

Miriam and Aaron went out to weed the garden plot they shared with several other families. Jochebed hoped hard work would ease some of their sorrow and anger. She considered the different reactions of her children to the news of their father. Aaron was bewildered, unable to grasp the reality of it. Miriam was angry—with Pharaoh, with the overseer, even with the Lord God. Both Aaron and Miriam were having their first experience with sorrow.

When it was time for the noonday meal, she went out to the garden. "You've worked all morning. Now come in to eat. I have a surprise for you; Lael brought us a cake with apricots and nuts in it."

"I'm not hungry." Miriam's tear-washed eyes sparkled with anger that her morning's work had not dissipated.

"Me neither." Aaron thought it couldn't be proper to enjoy anything now. He ran to the other side of the garden.

Jochebed reached for Miriam's hand and nodded toward Aaron. "Come with me."

The two walked to where Aaron sat on the east side of the garden plot, staring at nothing. When they sat down beside him, he didn't acknowledge their presence.

After a moment Jochebed began to talk to him, to Miriam, and to herself:

"Sometimes when our minds are suddenly filled with grief, we forget the better times we've had, and we don't let ourselves think of good times that surely will come yet. We must learn not to stretch present problems out in our mind until they swallow up everything else.

"Since we can think of only one thing at a time, we must try to think of your father's years of loving us and teaching us—the times of laughing . . . the times of playing . . . the times we heard him pray to the Lord God for us all. He would want us to do that.

"Dreadful things happen to everyone at some time or other. I wonder why we carry on so about it . . . as though heartbreak is unique, something that should have been avoided forever. We must remember this: Bitterness and anger and self-pity will only make our lives more weighted down. Those attitudes won't solve anything. We must fight them.

"It's all right to cry for a while, but life will go on, and we will find ways to put aside much of our present sorrow— just as your father would tell us to do.

"He would want us to keep on learning, working, and playing games and eating cakes with apricots and nuts whenever we can.

"Shall we go into the house now?"

Her words had a calming effect on each of them. Aaron found his voice. "If Father would want me to be happy, to learn, to work, to play, and to eat cakes . . . then I'll do it all!"

The little family walked back to the house, feeling closer to each other than ever before, each trying to be cheerful for the others—and for the father who would want it that way.

Jochebed's most pressing problem was what to do about her baby. She would not be able to hide him much longer. She believed the Lord God would protect her son, but she also believed it was important to do what one could in every circumstance. But what could she do in this one? At night when she should have been sleeping she too often lay awake thinking, worrying, trying to work out a plan.

On one such sleepless night after she had been teaching her children about Abraham and about the city of Ur of the Chaldees, which had once been his home, she remembered a legend Amram used to tell.

The story was of an ancient king of that region, whose name was Sargon. She didn't remember why Sargon's life was threatened when he was a baby, but that wasn't important now. What was important was so exciting it made her sit bolt upright in bed, fully awake! Sargon's mother, so the story went, wove a reed basket and covered it with tar. Then she put her child in it and set the basket in the gently flowing Euphrates. It drifted to where one named Akki sat on the riverbank. Akki rescued the child and raised him as his own. It was a wonderful story, a favorite of Amram's. He often told it to the children, and they grew wide-eyed as he dramatized the brief river voyage of the baby boy who grew up to be a king.

Now it was Jochebed who was wide-eyed at the story! She associated it with the small waterproofed papyrus boats she had seen Egyptian peasants using between the islands of the Nile. There were even larger papyrus boats that traversed the length of the great river. She would weave a baby-sized boat. Ophir would know how to get the pitch and tar to cover it. Then she would put her precious son in it and allow the basket-boat to drift—but to whom? Where? The crocodile-infested Nile was not as friendly a river as the Euphrates, and who would be their "Akki"?

She decided it was a useless idea, the desperate imagining of a mind that needed more sleep in order to think of a logical solution to her problem. Set her baby adrift on the Nile? Nonsense!

She was half amused and half annoyed at herself. How could she have given one serious thought to trusting the Nile—the crocodiles—and a fictitious Akki? She went to sleep.

Several times during the next morning she found herself thinking about a basket of papyrus floating with a tiny passenger. She knew of canals off the Nile that were not infested with crocodiles; there were small branches of the river where people swam in relative safety. There was even one place where everyone knew that the daughter of Rameses bathed. She would find a safe place like that for a small ark. Indeed, why not that very place? It was logical! If someone other than a member of the royal family found him, he would be turned over to the authorities immediately, but if the princess found him, Jochebed knew she would love him at once and would see that such a child must live. This beautiful child, whom she and Amram had dedicated to the Lord God before he was born, must live!

For three days she thought about it. The more she thought, the more reasonable it seemed. And since no other solution occurred to her, and since two more babies in the settlement had been taken away by soldiers in the last few weeks, she began making the basket. She asked Ophir to get the tar and pitch.

Carefully, lovingly, hopefully the basket-boat was made. When Miriam and Aaron asked what she was weaving, she told them it was to be a surprise. She wanted it to seem mysterious so her explanation, given at the proper time, would receive appropriate attention.

It was finished. She called Miriam and Aaron and told them to sit down because she had much to say to them. She began by telling them the old story of Sargon, not with Amram's high drama but with a feeling for the mother and the baby that made the story special in a different way.

As she spoke, Jochebed's small audience began to understand how that unusual basket would be used. And the story this time had an exciting sequel that included them.

"When we put our ark on the water, we'll place it in tall marsh grasses so it won't drift away. Miriam, you will stay nearby to watch over your brother. If you see any danger, call out; field workers near there will come to help. But if the princess comes to take the baby . . . let him go.

"Aaron, you will lie in the grass halfway between Miriam and the field workers so you can relay her call to them if that's necessary."

Their mother's idea was too great, too new; they could not accept it right away. They looked at each other, then at her—with obvious doubts.

But no doubts shadowed their mother's face. She had thought it over long enough. It was possible, probable, sensible and urgent. "We will do it today. It won't be any safer or easier if we wait until tomorrow."

She had gone through each step in her mind carefully, but nothing could prepare her for actually bundling her precious baby into the basket and releasing him to whatever would happen. She allowed herself to hold him close again. She kissed the top of his head and looked at his face—memorizing each feature.

Aaron held the basket, and Miriam held the small, thin

blanket. Jochebed took the blanket, wrapped her baby in it and gently laid him in his personal ark. She carried her treasure to the water's edge.

She had often told her children, "Do what you must do with as little fuss as possible." She also had often told them, "The more difficult a thing is, the better it is to get it over quickly." Never had her practical creed been more appropriate—or more difficult to implement.

She stooped, placed the basket in the water and gently pulled stalks of feathery papyrus reeds around it to keep it out of the current. Two ducks squawked their noisy disapproval, and a wild heron took flight.

She watched the little vessel bob slightly on the water for a minute that seemed to be an eternity. Then she turned almost absentmindedly to wave to Miriam, who had taken her place as watcher. She looked toward Aaron, standing on a little rise some distance away; she motioned for him to lie down. He could hear just as well when he was hidden by the grass, and it would be better if neither he nor Miriam could be seen by the princess.

She denied herself one last look back to the water and walked home. She would spend the next hours weaving her straw mats to sell. She would weave and wait—and pray.

————————————————————6

Pharaoh's daughter . . . saw the basket among the reeds and
sent her slave girl to get it.   *Exodus 2:5*

Miriam's temperament did not make waiting easy.
Her restlessness made the hours of watching seem longer
than they were. Although she wouldn't admit it even to
herself, she was frightened, too, at being part of a plan she
thought had little chance of working out right. Still, she
watched over the basket and its beloved, vulnerable contents
protectively and wouldn't have entrusted her assignment to
any other watcher.

The first indication that her vigil was ending startled her
even though she had been waiting for hours. She heard
women's voices, some of them laughing. Those happy
sounds only sent a stinging, stabbing pain to Miriam's
breast. Then as they came close enough for her to glimpse
their bright-colored robes, her panic increased. The next moments were the crucial ones.

Miriam settled down further into the grass but not before
she risked a last glance at the princess. Miriam never had
seen so lovely a lady. "Beautiful—beautiful—beautiful" was
all she could think. Meoris, perfectly groomed and lavishly
dressed, walked with the pride and grace of one who knew
she was royalty and thoroughly enjoyed that privilege.

Two of Meoris's slaves waded into the water to make
certain it was safe. The princess casually scanned the sky
and the river. "Adah, what is that strange basket over there?
Bring it to me."

Adah waded over to it. In astonishment she picked it up and without a word brought it to her mistress.

When the princess saw the handsome baby, she smiled; when the baby saw the princess, he cried.

At his cry Miriam instinctively responded to what she knew she must do—and do well! Her mouth felt so dry that she doubted she would be able to speak; she hoped the weakness that made getting to her feet difficult wouldn't be apparent to the princess. She was grateful she wasn't immediately noticed and relieved to find her confidence returning with each step she took.

Meoris, delightfully surprised, was telling Adah what the slave girl already knew. "This is one of the Hebrew babies." Meoris had put aside her usual unruffled poise. "How did he get in such a place? Who would put him there? And why would anyone *dare* choose this place when everyone knows it's reserved for the family of Rameses?" She had talked herself back into her accustomed attitude and tone of voice.

None of her maids offered an answer. They had learned that silence was safer than answers that displeased royalty.

She didn't need anyone's answers. When she saw Miriam approaching, she understood. The baby was put in that exact spot by a desperate family. Obviously they intended that he be found by a particular person who could save him from a very different encounter with the Nile. Meoris felt a rapport with such a daring family—especially with the lovely dark-haired girl coming to meet her and trying to hide her fears and self-consciousness. Meoris instantly decided that she liked her.

As Miriam had practiced in her mind during her watch, she bowed and asked permission to speak.

Meoris was amused at this incredible drama. "Speak, girl, if you know anything about this baby."

Miriam's voice was filled with love and pride. "This baby almost never cries, unless he's hungry or frightened. And he's very hungry now, for he's been in that basket a long time."

She paused to catch her breath, and seeing that Meoris appeared interested, she found the courage to speak her last rehearsed line. "I . . . I know where to find a Hebrew woman who would nurse him . . . if you want her to."

Meoris was enchanted by the girl's concern for this baby, who obviously was her brother. She was certain the nurse Miriam spoke of was not far away and was hoping to be called to care for this baby, who would be no stranger to her.

"I have heard you. I will think about what I will do. Wait here." The princess, carrying the crying infant, walked to the river and stepped out into it. The water was refreshing, but only a short distance away it became a place of horror. She knew her father's law about male Hebrew babies, but she wondered whether it could matter to him if just this one wasn't killed. He wouldn't care about only one boy child, and if he did, she could charm him into making an exception for her. She would do it.

She called to Miriam, "I have decided. Go. Get a nurse who will take good care of this baby for me."

Miriam thought to herself, She will take care of him for *us*, not for *you*, and my parents believe "us" means a lot of people! But aloud she said only what Princess Meoris expected to hear: "As you say, I will do. I will run; she will be ready. Shall I bring her here, to this place?"

"I will be here. I'll bathe and then lie in the sun until you come back."

Miriam first ran to where Aaron waited and called for him to run home with her. She told him the news as they ran.

They burst into their house and found their mother praying. She looked up at the faces of her children and read the answer to her prayer in their eyes.

Meoris called out to the baby's family as they hurried toward her. "I've named him Moses because I drew him out of the water."

Jochebed bowed. As soon as she caught her breath she said, "Moses . . . is a good name. In our language, too, it means 'draw out.' "

"What is your name?"

"I am Jochebed, wife of Amram, who serves Pharaoh at Abu Simbel. This is my daughter, Miriam, and this is my son, Aaron."

The children bowed, but Meoris took no notice of them. "Jochebed, take this baby and nurse him for me and I will pay you well. Moses will receive official protection and a generous allowance and, in time, an education appropriate for a prince of Egypt.

"Here is my signet ring. If you want anything for the child, send it to me with a message of what you need."

The moment Jochebed took her son into her arms he looked up at her face, snuggled to her breast and fell asleep.

Meoris gave one quick nod of her head. She was satisfied. "I will send my messenger from time to time to check on the boy. Moses will be brought to me whenever I want to see him."

"As you wish."

"Good. Now, Jochebed, tell Adah how to find your house so my servants can know the way to find my son."

Meoris ordered her attendants to sing and dance; she joined in with them. She had claimed a son, so they must celebrate.

When they started back to the palace, she looked at Adah in mock concern. "Tell me—can you imagine the look on my father's face if he finds out what I've done?"

Adah said, "Yes, my princess, I can." Adah couldn't cope with the vision of a furious Pharaoh as easily as Meoris did; the slave girl did not smile.

Meoris hummed a favorite melody. She was delighted that because of her one handsome Hebrew baby boy would have a royal upbringing and would be considered part of Pharaoh's household. Pharaoh's daughter laughed softly and shook her head in amazement. This child might even be Egypt's Pharaoh one day! Lord of the Diadem, King of Upper and Lower Egypt, Beloved of Ptah—the Pharaoh's titles were grandiose. Her expression changed as she thought of the names he would have been called—had he even survived—if he had one day been part of a slave crew.

Crude, demeaning names were hurled at slaves to antagonize them and to amuse the bored overseers. And his face and back, his arms and legs would have been scarred by the whips of taskmasters, who considered Hebrews expendable in order to meet their work quotas.

She knew she had made the right choice.

That night Moses slept in his own bed as his family talked of the day just ending. They had gone over the details of it many times, and with each telling it became more wonderful.

Aaron yawned and Miriam's eyes were partly closed. It was time for their mother to say, "We must go to bed now; we're all tired. But first, we will give thanks to the Lord God for His blessings.

"O Lord, everlasting Lord, we praise You for Your loving-kindness and Your faithfulness. Teach us day by day what we should do, and let Your favor rest on us as we are obedient to You. May holiness adorn our house, O Lord, everlasting Lord."

_____7

So the woman took the baby and nursed him.   *Exodus 2:9*

Meoris's messenger arrived five days later, early in the morning. Jochebed heard the chariot clattering down the stony street; it stopped in front of her house. She was thankful to the Lord God that this time her house would be entered by someone who was ordered to protect Moses, not to kill him. She ran to open the door.

"Jochebed, wife of Amram?"

"Yes."

"Is the child, Moses, here?"

"Yes. Do you want to see him?"

"Not necessary. I am merely to tell you that Princess Meoris wishes Moses in a different location, closer to the palace. She has arranged for him—also for you and your daughter and your son. Tomorrow. Be ready to move. Take only personal things; your new quarters will be well furnished. Do you have questions?"

"No questions, sir."

"You will be ready tomorrow?"

"Tomorrow."

He was gone. The wheels of the chariot rolled noisily over the street, and when the sound of it faded away she said, "Just like that! As if it were nothing! 'Be ready tomorrow. Any questions?' " Jochebed wasn't sure if she had said it aloud or only in her mind.

She paced the floor, then sat down deliberately with her back to the door. In earlier years that door was open to relatives. Amram's brothers—Ishar, Hebron and Uzziel—

used to bring their families; their children played with Miriam and Aaron while the adults talked of problems and pleasures—whatever was worth talking about. That door had also been open to friends—Gether and Hannah, Ophir and Lael, and Uzal. But in the last years those occasions had been rare. People no longer had time or strength to socialize. Families lost touch with each other, and the news they had to discuss only made them more depressed.

Recently, that door had been forced open several times by the king's soldiers, sent to search for a baby boy. Ophir had come through it to tell her about Amram. And now it had admitted one who said she must leave her house tomorrow. And so she chose to sit with her back to the door—the door through which she would walk for the last time in just a few hours.

Since there was no one with whom to talk it over, she resorted to "thought talk"—her description of how she reasoned verbally but silently with herself. It had been a lifelong habit on which she had been relying more frequently since Amram was gone.

"And so, you leave two rooms filled with shabby things. Is that so bad?

"What if the messenger had come to say Meoris had changed her mind, revoked her protection, wanted the signet ring back? What if he had stepped aside to let soldiers in to take Moses?"

That was enough! She got up, ran to the door and pounded it with her fists to release the frustration she couldn't justify any longer. Then she pushed that door open—to let in more light while she began to pack a few things.

She looked so happy that neither her son nor her daughter wanted to say that they very much preferred to stay

Miriam and Aaron came in from the garden. She set out bread and cheese and cucumbers. As they ate, she told them they were going to move to a better house the next day; Meoris had arranged it. There was not much conversation while they ate.

After lunch was over, Jochebed handed her children large baskets and told them to pack their belongings, then find any of their friends they could and bid them good-bye.

She scooped Moses out of his bed to take him with her as she went to call on neighbors to tell them her news and to offer them articles she wouldn't need any longer—lamps, benches, dishes, pitchers—dear, familiar things.

There was no time to get word to relatives, so she asked neighbors to let them know when they could. "Tell them we've moved by order of the house of Pharaoh. The messenger said only that we will be closer to the palace. I'll try to find a way to let you know where we are. And . . . if . . . Amram comes home . . . tell him, too."

Jochebed and her children had spread the news, had given away belongings that had suddenly become unnecessary, and had packed up the few possessions they would take with them. Finally, physically and emotionally exhausted, they tossed mats on the floor and lay down to sleep.

In the darkness Aaron's voice, with more joy in it than he had shown during their entire busy day, said, "It's all right, Mother; I'm sure Father would want us to go to this better place."

It was as though Jochebed heard the encouraging voice of Amram. "Thank you, Aaron. I, too, think he would want this, and he would be pleased with how you and Miriam are helping to make the move easier for me. Now sleep well."

In the dark each one could cry sentimental tears in privacy. No one could tell whether the others slept or kept a vigil in the house that held many, many memories that would never be put to rest.

When the messenger returned the next morning, they were ready. They and their modest bundles were loaded into splendid royal chariots. Aaron carried his most prized possession—a ball made of hide, which his father had stuffed and stitched for him. Miriam, Aaron and Jochebed wore their papyrus sandals and linen tunics that were saved for special occasions. The group that gathered to wave good-bye was small; most of the neighbors were at work—making bricks for a fortress.

Some of the men treading vats of clay mixture that day remembered that Amram believed his newborn son was marked for greatness. They wondered if perhaps the unexplainable thing happening now did have some significance. Some began to hope.

Jochebed and her family had never ridden in a chariot before and found their journey an exciting delight. They had no idea of the number of miles they had gone, but they knew when the chariot turned onto a long lane that they were at their destination. They rode through the main gate of a high, thick stone wall; the estate inside the wall was like a small town.

The first building they saw was a private temple for the worship of the family's gods. Next was the mansion—an immense three-story building with a roof terrace. It was surrounded by carefully landscaped flower beds, three small pools half full of lotus blossoms and one larger pool for swimming—secluded by tamarisk and willow trees. Beyond the swimming pool and its lovely grove of trees was an assortment of buildings. One was their new house, standing with more than a dozen others built for servant families. There was a well, a building that housed a kitchen with several ovens, a slaughter house, two grain silos, stables for ten horses and two chariots. Beyond the buildings were acres of vegetable gardens, orchards and vineyards.

The "town" was self-contained. It belonged to Rekhmire, the chief superintendent of river mouths, and was appropriate for one with so important a position in the delta region.

It was unheard of that slaves arrived in a royal chariot or even were allowed to enter through the main gate. It was surprising that Jochebed's house was the largest in the servants' compound, while her family was the smallest in number. The nicely furnished five-room house and the new clothing for Jochebed and her children in baskets arranged on shelves were beyond the little family's highest hopes.

Jochebed accepted these tokens of Meoris's promised provision gratefully—as coming from El Shaddai!

Miriam and Aaron were assigned to work in the vegetable
gardens; the normal work day was from sunup until sundown. They were reminded, "Although you belong to a
favored slave family, you must work hard and well."

They were disappointed. Having received so much already, the brother and sister of Meoris's adopted son felt
they were entitled to more.

Jochebed continued to weave some mats, but her chief
responsibility was caring for Moses. Her heart sang. Protected by Pharaoh's own family, she would raise her son for
the God of Abraham, Isaac and Jacob. As soon as he was
able to learn, she would teach him of the one God and of
His promise to bless all nations of the whole world through
the descendants of Abraham. He would know the One to
whom he ultimately belonged—not to her or to Meoris but
to that God whose names are descriptions of His being: Elohim—the Creator God; Yahweh—He who causes to be; El
Shaddai—God Almighty; Yahweh-yireh—the Lord will provide!

Meoris seldom sent for Moses in those early years, but
her servant came regularly to check on him and to remind
Jochebed that the house of Rameses had a claim on him.

As the baby grew into a sturdy toddler, he became the
pet of most of the other slaves in their compound. At times
he was indulged even by the mistress of the great house—
given sweets and allowed to ride in a miniature chariot built
especially for her own children.

The children of the great house enjoyed their private
swimming pool and played with their pet dogs and mon-
keys. Jochebed's children splashed in a canal and played
with a lanky dog that belonged to the garden overseer and
a cat that attached herself to their household.

Rekhmire bought his children fascinating toys. They had
painted wooden dolls, metal dwarfs that danced on a small
platform when strings were pulled, and a copper cat that

would open its mouth at the tug of a string. Jochebed showed Moses how to play with sticks and stones and mud.

Life was easier for Jochebed than she ever dreamed it could be, and yet there were great restless moods that frequently overcame her joy and gladness. She missed Amram so very much and wondered if he were well—or even alive. And she thought of her family and friends in Pithom and Rameses and other places with no respite from the burdens heaped on them by the rulers of Mizraim.

Her children often heard her pray: "Lord God, You will not forsake us nor let us be destroyed nor forget the covenant made with our fathers. Let Your servants hear Your voice, and let them be obedient."

8

May your deeds be shown to your servants, your splendor to
their children.   *Psalm 90:16*

They had lived for seven years in what they still
called their "new" quarters. Jochebed used each year well.
She nurtured her son with love and lullabies and with stories
of his own father and his forefathers. The young child's
favorite was the story of Joseph. Jochebed wondered if it
appealed to him because Joseph, too, was a favored son,
envied by his brothers and destined for greatness.

During planting or harvesting Aaron and Miriam did the
seasonal tasks. At planting time they worked the heavy
wood plow with a team of indifferent cows. Miriam led and
pulled at the animals with a rope; Aaron guided the plow
with one hand and scattered seeds with the other. A very
young slave, about Moses' age, followed them to cover the
seeds lightly with the rich, black soil. The work was hard;
the hot sun rose too early and set too late.

"Will it never end, this drudgery on these acres?" Miriam
felt she must do something about the situation, even if it
was only to fuss about things.

"You might hope it won't end, Miriam. These overseers
are demanding, but not cruel. Can't you be thankful you
aren't in Pithom——making bricks or carrying water to half-
dead slaves . . . or any of a dozen other things, even worse,
that your sisters are forced to do?" Aaron had determined
from the time Amram was taken away to be as much like
his father as possible, even in the difficult task of accepting
his lot by doing the most excellent job possible.

Miriam said no more to him, but that evening, still full
of resentment, she spoke to her mother. "How soon do you
think Moses can go with us to work in the fields?"

"He's only seven years old!"

"He could follow Aaron and me to cover seeds with soil. He could pull weeds. He might even . . ."

"It doesn't do any good to ask me, Miriam. I'm not the one to decide what work Moses will do or when he will do it. Princess Meoris does. She even may decide to take him away from us."

"I don't think she will do that. She doesn't seem to want him for more than short diversions, and not even for that very often."

Jochebed was tired, and talking about Meoris made her uneasy. She got up from her bench, stretched and even managed a yawn to indicate that their discussion was over.

The visions that had come to Miriam's mind were clearer to her than her mother's hints to be quiet. "Suppose Princess Meoris does take Moses. Suppose some day he is in a high position at court. Will he see to it that we are well provided for?"

"Miriam, Miriam, . . . listen to me, dear." Jochebed could not hide a subtle tone of self-pity as she reluctantly resumed their conversation. "I know how it is to be a slave. . . . I've been one all my life, and I've worked hard for scant pay. I have . . . for these many years . . . even lost my husband to Pharaoh's labor force at Abu Simbel. And it's even more heartbreaking for me to see my children enslaved than to suffer it myself. But . . . I wouldn't trade Moses for my freedom—or yours or Aaron's."

She bit her lip, hesitating to say any more, then decided to add one more thing: "Miriam, you're a beautiful young woman with a mind filled with dreams . . . and a desperate urgency for them to come true. Always be high-spirited. Always look toward a better time. As long as you can hope, you are not totally a slave."

Miriam doubted that her mother ever felt the frustration she did; it was so intense that any "hope" of something better only made present things worse by comparison.

"Good night, Mother. It will take more than words to keep me from feeling like a slave when I'm back in the fields tomorrow . . . sweating and tired."

Jochebed ached to hold her daughter in her arms and tuck her into bed, as she had done years before. It's easier to comfort a child than to give solace to a slave.

Planting time had ended. The crops flourished and were ready to harvest. Aaron and Miriam, armed with sickles, reaped stalks of grain to be sent to the threshing floor, separated with forks and winnowed.

Miriam's back hurt and her arms ached, but she wouldn't mention it to Aaron. He would just tell her to be glad they had no whip-wielding taskmasters to make their backs hurt more. And she wouldn't tell her mother how she felt; her mother would talk about hope and high spirits. Miriam was too depressed for philosophy.

Miriam's comment that previous spring about the possibility of Moses' becoming an integral part of Pharaoh's household had a sharp impact on Jochebed. She had become used to her comparatively comfortable situation, but now she realized she must make every day an important step in establishing Moses firmly in the faith of his fathers. He must learn more than basic stories of the patriarchs; he must learn their significance. He must learn, most of all, of Elohim.

Jochebed "thought talked" for a while. "This should have been Amram's responsibility and privilege! Or, with Amram away, one of Moses' uncles should be near to teach him of the one God and how to worship Him."

Then she reminded herself of her rule against regret with its resulting waste of time and energy. She would give her son as thorough a training as it was possible for her to give. She spent time with him every day, telling familiar stories—but with added emphasis.

When she told him about Joseph, she now taught that he grew up to be a powerful leader in Egypt by El Shaddai's specific design and that only through God-given wisdom was Joseph able to make Egypt prosper and to save much of the world—including the Hebrew nation—from starving.

Moses learned the important, timely promise that the Lord God gave to Abraham—that his descendants would be out of their land for 400 years. He experienced excitement, as only a child can, in knowing that a time was coming when the Lord God would make a way for them to return to the land He had given them. Moses didn't know much about Canaan, but he was ready to go there, for his mother spoke of it with delight. She told him all she had heard of its beauty and its fruitfulness.

Jochebed taught him that when the Lord God chooses a person to be His servant, He calls him and leads and enables him. He did that for Abraham, Jacob and Joseph. He would do it for the one chosen for His next important work.

Moses found the history of his people fascinating. He also learned that by asking for "one more story" he could postpone bedtime. Jochebed recognized the tactic but welcomed it, for it gave her opportunities to reinforce in his impressionable mind his heritage of courage and his privilege of belonging to the one God.

She quenched any interest he might have had in Egyptian gods. "The Nile is only a river; the sun is our God's gift of light and warmth. Birds and animals are just birds and animals. There is no such thing as a man with an animal's head, or an animal with a man's head . . . except those made of stone or metal. And stone and metal are only stone and metal, nothing more."

She even dared tell him that Pharaoh, who sat on a high throne with people bowing in fear in front of him, was just a man—just like his father was and like Aaron was becoming and like Moses himself would be one day.

"And, Moses, remember: The God we worship created the Nile, the birds, the animals, the stones and trees and metals, the earth and the sky—and all mankind. There is just one God—Elohim!"

She knew Moses could not understand all this yet, but with the tools of repetition and consistency she taught him there were only two ways of life: one lived for false gods, the other lived for the almighty, everlasting, most high God.

Moses knew from earliest childhood that the most high God was jealous of His children and would not tolerate any claim on them except His own.

9

When the child grew older, she took him to Pharaoh's daughter.   *Exodus 2:10*

The seven-year-old became eight, nine, and then ten. Meoris seldom asked for him. Jochebed was glad, for she didn't want the boy to become entranced with the exotic life of the royal household. The court's pageantry, the wizards' magic, the dissipation and hedonistic entertainments of the royal banquets, luxurious ease as a normal way of life, and even the grotesque idols could all become hypnotic enticements that a boy might find too much to resist. She felt threatened by the influence that Mizraim's morals and culture could have on him, even on short visits into its realm.

She taught him simple things—to study weather signs in the sky and to identify plants and trees. He helped her weave multicolored mats of fine design. But she would not send him into the fields unless she was ordered to do it by Meoris.

They had time for conversations about such things as the sacred writings: "Men guard with their lives the writings that have been handed down through generations of our people. One day, when you learn to read, you will find your uncles, and they will tell you where the writings are. Maybe you can read them yourself.

"No other people can trace their ancestry back to the beginning of time. The Hebrews are excellent record keepers; the Lord God requires it of them."

"Can all the Hebrews write in these records?"

"No, only those men the Lord God chooses to do it."

"How do they know what to write?"

"The Lord God tells them."

"I don't believe it."

"Moses, . . . there's another word you can use instead of *believe*. Try saying 'I don't *understand* it.' "

"What's the difference?"

"The difference is . . . that you can believe what you can't understand." She thought for a time about how to say this best to a 10-year-old and tried again to make the point. "Think about a grain of wheat. Aaron plants it and believes it will sprout and turn into a tall plant with many grains. Does he understand how this comes from one planted kernel?"

"No."

"But he *believes* it will, so he plants the seed. Now if our God can perform that kind of miracle millions of times in a growing season—and can do other miracles we see every day without stopping to think about most of them—it's not hard to believe He can put into a man's mind what to write . . . even the words to use."

The boy seemed unimpressed. "It's easier to think about planting than about God's putting His words into men's minds and then getting them written down."

Jochebed laughed and answered, "Of course it is. But the reason for that is . . . you are 10 years old. When you are older, your mind will think greater thoughts, just as your legs and arms will improve in what they can do."

"By the time I'm 12?"

"Possibly." She gave him a hug and sent him off to join some children who were having a relay race, putting more energy into the screaming than into the game. She watched him go with approval. His arms and his legs—and his mind—did work quite well already.

By the time Moses was 12 he had learned to say the names of his ancestors in order, the way some children say the alphabet or the multiplication tables: "Adam, Seth, Enosh, Kenan, Mahalalel, Jared, Enoch, Methuselah, Lamech, Noah, Shem, Arphaxad, Shelah, Eber, Peleg, Reu, Serug,

Nahor, Terah, Abraham, Isaac, Jacob, Levi, Kohath, Amram."

He knew their names, the meaning of each name, and how each had been important in the Lord God's plan in his own generation. He was proud to have his own father's name in such a list. Jochebed told her son that his father's contribution to his people was in being a man of great faith and fervent prayer and in being one of the Lord God's best witnesses and encouragers to his generation. And he sired three children, each one dedicated to the Lord God.

One day, after reciting the names and accomplishments of the men, he asked with a puzzled look, "Will the list end with Amram's name?"

"No. There is already a generation after Amram's."

"That's my generation!"

"Yes. And the man God chooses from your generation will have to be a very special person—very, very special." She had never given Moses cause to think that she felt he was to be God's next prophet. If it were so, God would make it known to him at the proper time.

"Why will this new man have to be so special?"

"You know why! I've told you many times. Your generation will be privileged to see the prophecy given to Abraham fulfilled. God will call a strong, wise, obedient man to lead His people home to Canaan."

"Will this man be greater than Abraham or Jacob?"

"I can't answer such a question, but I do know he will love his own people with a deep love, and they will remember him and honor him in all time to come, and he will be blessed by the Lord God."

Jochebed heard the wheels of a chariot and instinctively knew that Meoris was sending for Moses again. He enjoyed his rare visits to the palace more than she enjoyed having him go.

The chariot wheels ceased clattering, and she walked toward the back door to call Moses. Then she heard a second chariot coming, and she stopped short. Her first thought was that this other chariot must have brought the princess.

She always hoped Meoris would come one time. They had not seen each other for 12 years, yet devoted to the same boy, they had much in common despite their backgrounds. Jochebed smoothed her hair as she turned and went to the front door.

She recognized the messenger but not the two porters with him. There had not been porters before. Moses packed nothing to take on his visits; he had a complete wardrobe at the palace.

She looked beyond the men who were walking toward her to the second chariot. It was empty, except for the driver.

The three men were now within speaking range, and the messenger said, "Jochebed! Princess Meoris has decided. This time Moses will not return here. She sends her compliments to you on raising him to be a strong, healthy boy."

He went on talking but Jochebed scarcely heard him.

"She wants you to know she will keep her word about educating Moses as a prince of Egypt; he will attend the best schools. In time he may be allowed to visit you. You and your children may stay on this estate indefinitely . . . as long as you make no trouble.

"Now! Direct the porters to the things Moses will want to take with him."

And so the moment she had expected for 12 years had finally come. It was not as violent an experience as she had sometimes imagined it would be; instead, it had an eerie quality of unreality. She heard herself saying, "As the princess has said, so it will be."

She showed them a few articles to put in the ridiculously oversized chest they had brought. Then she went again toward the back door to call Moses. She tried to call, but she had no voice.

The messenger hurried past her out of the door. Moses was walking back from the stable area, and the royal servant ran to meet him.

Jochebed watched as they talked briefly to each other. Then she saw Moses guided toward the road where the chariots waited. She ran to the front door as terror assaulted her in a sickening surge.

The porters loaded her son's belongings into the first chariot; they boarded it and signaled for the driver to leave for the palace. The messenger walked with Moses to the other chariot, and as his charge stepped into it, he bowed low to the son of Meoris.

The woman who had experienced the loneliness and heavy responsibility of widowhood, even though her husband still lived, now felt bereaved of her beloved son, even though he, too, would live on.

She stood frozen, waiting to see Moses swept from her sight without even a good-bye—just as Amram had been taken. Instead, the messenger ran back to her.

"Jochebed!" She had heard him say her name many times, and he always made it sound like a command. "The son of Pharaoh's daughter wishes you to ride to the palace with him. You will be brought back here before sundown."

She didn't stop even to smooth her hair again but ran to where Moses waited. She had ridden in a chariot only once—when they had come to this place more than 12 years before. It was that long ago that she had offered her son to Pharaoh's daughter, and now the transaction was to be completed.

As she rode the few miles with him to the palace, she kept thinking of things to tell him. Almost every sentence began with "Remember!" or "Don't forget!"

On the way back from the palace there was no one in the chariot to talk to, so she "thought talked."

"I've been given 12 years with him . . . 12 more than there might ever have been. What right do I have to think I should have had more?

"He may visit me; the messenger said so.

"I may yet see my son called by the Lord God to lead our people. How much I have to be thankful for . . . and to look forward to!"

Meoris did keep her word. Jochebed's family remained on Rekhmire's estate; Moses was allowed to visit after a whole year had passed.

When he came, he talked about his school. "I'm learning to read very well, Mother."

"Good. One day you can read the records of the Hebrews."

"I'm learning arithmetic and science."

"Good. Your mind is growing; I told you it would."

"I'm meeting boys of my own age, and we have good times together."

"It's fine to be happy. Everything you have said pleases me, but tell me, Moses, do you go to the Egyptian temples?"

"I have to learn about storm gods, sky gods, river gods . . . all kinds of gods."

"There is *one* God! Only one!"

"Mother, I respect Princess Meoris and belong to her by law. It pleases her when I talk of her gods and when I go to ceremonies at the temple. I'm not allowed even to speak of our God."

"But neither the princess nor all her priests and tutors will erase what I've impressed on your mind already, and your own good sense will tell you not to worship the nongods of Mizraim!"

"I didn't say I worship Egyptian gods; I said I'm learning about them, and I sometimes go to the temple with my princess. Can't I do that and still worship our God?"

Jochebed gave his question careful thought. "That's a hard question. . . . I believe giving idols even polite, implied respect is wrong, but for now . . . I know . . . you must be obedient to Meoris.

"Just remember . . . remember the warnings our fathers have been given about other gods.

"And, don't forget . . . every day . . . praise our Lord God for the privileges and opportunities you have been given; pray to Him to keep you from being turned aside from Him by people who scorn Him because they don't know Him.

"And, most especially, Moses . . . listen to me . . . there will come a time when you will find it's impossible to be both Egyptian and Hebrew.

"Meanwhile, learn everything you can about reading and writing. Learn arithmetic and the sciences. Learn all your mind can hold of such things. This kind of knowledge is treasure."

"Knowledge is treasure." Moses thought of his mother's words often—on mornings when he felt too exhausted to get up to go to his daily sessions with the priests and tutors of the school at On and during evenings when he was too tired to write one more stroke or read one more word in preparation for the next day's work.

Still, if knowledge was treasure, he would mine it for his people and somehow use it for their good. He would have to! How else could he justify the years of fine living and being educated in the best schools, when other Hebrews knew nothing but the agony and despair of slavery. His situation and theirs were as opposite as darkness and light, yet he—in a very real way—was in bondage, too. His days were long; his assignments were heavy; and his tutors were strict. He belonged to the house of Rameses—but he was barred from his own home. His intense preoccupation with his studies kept him from dwelling on this too much, but a very basic part of him was increasingly dissatisfied.

---10

. . . and he became her son. *Exodus 2:10*

Moses became Meoris's life. She not only loved him but also intended to make her investment in him pay very well. Through him, when her father was dead, she planned to rule Egypt. She determined that Moses' education would be second to none; then she would manipulate his future with her innate expertise in diplomacy.

She liked to remember the day she went to the Nile with her attendants and discovered a basket that held the most beautiful baby boy she had ever seen. Even when his tiny face was distorted by lusty cries, he had a captivating charm. Meoris didn't care much for babies, but this one was different. The moment she saw him, it was as if she were his slave forever, devoted to his well-being. As soon as she had taken him in her arms, she knew she could not resign him to the certain death that would claim him in that absurd little boat. If it didn't capsize with the wriggling infant or drift downstream to the sacred crocodiles, then certainly its tiny occupant would die of starvation or terror.

She had made claiming him seem a whimsical lark to her maidservants, but she secretly shared Adah's dread of angering her father. She insisted that all of them should dance and sing because that eased her tensions and gave her a sense that all would be well.

She often wondered how she had found the courage to do what she did. It was easy to whisk a baby from a basket, but as she held him, crying and clinging to her, she disciplined herself to see her responsibility—and danger—if she saved the child.

In incidental matters such as lavish barge journeys on the Nile or a splendid three-day party to entertain a hundred of her friends she had no difficulty persuading her father to indulge her. But she had no delusions about the problem it would be to get him to make an exception to the one rule that he enforced as though it were the key to his empire's survival—the rule that no Hebrew baby boy might live. If she angered him, not only would she see this handsome child die, but she could also lose her high favor with her father.

Meoris knew that the decrees making the Hebrews slaves and calling for male infants to be annihilated were prompted by more than Rameses' envy of their former prosperity or his fear that they might collaborate with some unlikely invader. He was motivated, unknowingly, by the priests of On. They fed his envy and his apprehensions about the Hebrews with false prophecies and insinuations of imminent insurrection. In spite of her father's strong will and his well-developed intelligence, the thoughts he claimed as his own often were put in his mind by the self-serving priests of On.

Meoris was not naive. Her father was sentimental toward her only to a point; beyond that there was a ruthlessness that would vent itself even on his favorite daughter if he considered her disloyal or if he thought one of her requests was an affront to his wisdom.

She quickly decided not to challenge him but to hide the baby.

It had been no problem to keep Moses safe and her father unaware of him in the early years. She simply released him to his mother for the best of care and had him and his family moved to the home of one of her few trusted friends for utmost safety. Pharaoh would send no soldiers to hunt for a Hebrew boy child in the prestigious home of Rekhmire, the superintendent of river mouths. And not one of Rekhmire's slaves would inform because of the announced penalty of a life for a life if it were done. Rekhmire made few rules, but those he made were notably enforced without exception, and he did not hesitate to discipline swiftly and severely—not only the offender but also the offender's family.

Meoris seldom saw Moses in his early years—only a few times when her father was off on a trip and once when she made a pilgrimage to Sais, the city of the goddess Neith, and had the boy brought to her there.

Because of the need for strict secrecy, she did not fully enjoy his visits, and because what pleasure she did derive from seeing him was not worth the danger to him or to herself, she rarely sent for him. But her personal messenger had been dispatched to Rekhmire's estate often to make certain that Moses was getting along well.

She knew Jochebed would take good care of him. She had risked her own life and the lives of her other two children to protect him in his infancy. Meoris was accustomed to seeing people use people, not risk their lives because of love for them. Rameses' family was made up of many enemies, each vying for his throne. She admired the family of Jochebed more than she would admit.

During the years Moses was cared for by his mother, Meoris developed grand plans for him. Those plans could not be implemented by Jochebed, for she knew nothing of the court manners he must learn and couldn't begin to educate him as royalty should be educated.

And so when he was old enough and Meoris had made arrangements, she ordered him taken from his family. It still was not safe for him to be in the palace, so she enrolled him without undue attention in the school at On where many of her father's harem children were students. Her plan had worked beautifully. Moses had adapted well to the first phase of his education for a place of authority.

Now it was time to advance her plan. She requested an audience with her father.

Rameses reserved a special expression for Meoris—a blend of joy, pride and delight. She was pleased to see that familiar look on his face as she walked toward his throne. She bowed to the ruler of Egypt. But she smiled up at her father like a trusting child.

"What is it you wish this time, fairest daughter of Egypt?"

She pretended a reluctance to speak in order to arouse his interest—a reversal of her usual eager response to his generous-sounding questions.

"Speak, Meoris. Are you thinking of a golden barge for a long trip on the Nile? Or only a trained black panther with a jeweled collar? Perhaps another summer house?" He was in an indulgent mood and phrased questions that spoke of his own present desires.

"My father, this time I am thinking of you . . . what I desire is for you."

"Something for *me?*" He looked ecstatic.

"Yes. Since you have not decided on a suitable successor for the exalted royal Throne of Geb . . ."

"*Silence!*" He interrupted what he regarded as insolence. His hands clenched the arms of his throne chair. He stiffened his back, and his eyes narrowed. His voice assumed a grim pomposity. "From sons of my great wives I am considering three princes: Kha, Emwise and Merneptah. And *you know this!*"

Meoris was more frightened than she had ever been before, but she steadied her voice and continued her plea.

"O great Son of Re, Offspring of Amon, Ruler of the World from the Fourth Cataract to the Euphrates . . . may I suggest you delay choosing from those favored sons because you do not find in them one worthy to be successor to so superior a Pharaoh as Rameses the Great? You have told me, O Mighty One, that you were your father's coregent before you were the age of the youngest of those three." Meoris wouldn't dignify them by repeating their names.

Rameses was still angry. His daughter's words, designed to restore his wounded pride, had not been effectual. The throne room throbbed with tense silence. No one moved except the tall Nubian attendant, the Fan Bearer on the King's Right Hand. He kept the white ostrich feathers stirring the air with a perpetual rhythm that now seemed an intrusion into the crisis Meoris had created. The Pharaoh had executed people for insubordination of far less magnitude than hers.

"Woman offspring of Golden Horus, King of Egypt, *do not meddle in my affairs!*" His voice roared.

Meoris had one more device to use—tears. They had been effective in bargaining with her father ever since she was a child, and this time the tears were real. "I am unmarried, and so I am unable to provide the son who might ascend to the Throne of Geb in my place. Because of this, I have a reasonable request to make, one that would let my father provide Egypt with the finest possible ruler to succeed Rameses . . . *the Great!*"

Pharaoh tilted his head to one side, looking skeptically at the stately woman who knelt weeping at his throne. She had challenged his authority and wisdom, but he was curious to know what plan she had. Meoris's ideas were sometimes foolish—but always interesting. He discounted the tears this time but said, "I will listen."

"I want to adopt a son. He must be an extraordinary one to follow so illustrious a ruler as Rameses. I want to be allowed to search for the most promising young man in Egypt. My investigation will be thorough, but the final choice will be yours, my father."

The ruler of Egypt stood silent, pondering the impact of Meoris's request on his family and his nation. He began to speak slowly, making her plan his own.

"You must do this. The priests will recommend young men. Also the army officers and my high officials will provide you with the names of those who might be worthy. You must interview them all. You must have great patience to do this important work well."

"As you say, I will do."

Meoris answered her agitated father's summons to the throne room two months later. When she bowed before him, he shouted, "You have been trying for months to decide on a boy to adopt. How long will it take you? I will do it myself!"

"My father, as we agreed, the final decision is to be yours, of course. The delay is that I haven't wanted to waste your valuable time in having to decide between the good and the very best. My judgment and intuition helped me weed out many, but I want to bring you only the finest of all."

Meoris's eyes danced. She leaned toward her father as though her next words were so confidential that she didn't want even his aides to hear. "I'm certain I've found that excellent one, but I will interview five of the best again just to make certain. It should not be long before I can present a young man for your approval."

"Not long? How long?"

"Two weeks."

"Not one more day than two weeks from today! The great wives are interceding for Kha, Emwise and Merneptah. I will make an end to all of this—-in two weeks!"

Rameses stalked out of the room, leaving a smiling daughter whose plans were working according to her schedule.

She recalled four of the most exceptional young men she had interviewed. She talked with each one briefly before dismissing them with a great show of appreciation and praise for their intelligence and charm.

Then she sent for Moses.

The day Moses was brought into the palace, she could not disguise her joy. The young man who stood in front of her was taller than she. His years of being set apart from other slaves for special treatment had given him confidence and a feeling of superiority that was evident in the way he stood, in the way he walked, in his conversation, and most of all in the way he had come to think of himself as destined for great things. She had intended for this to happen, and now she would continue to build his self-esteem even more. He would be the best-educated young man in Egypt; he already was the most handsome! She had ordered him a royal wardrobe; his attendants would be sensitive to his slightest need or desire. He would learn that it is essential to assume total authority. He must be master of those beneath him, which included everyone—even herself. He must defer only to Pharaoh, and Moses could learn the fine arts of flattery and subtlety to influence even him. Meoris would teach him the importance of politics.

Her mind whirled with plans, immediate and future. Then she realized she hadn't even spoken to him yet!

"Moses! Welcome to your home." Her smile was warm, and with a wide sweep of both arms she indicated that the sumptuous palace was his!

"You won't ever be going back to Rekhmire's estate. Forget everything there. You are the envy of every Egyptian boy. Tomorrow you will be presented to the Pharaoh, but his approval is a mere technicality. This is the moment I've waited for since the day Adah brought me the papyrus basket."

Moses knew well the story of the papyrus basket, and the mention of it made him think of his family. It was possible for the most envied boy in Egypt to be homesick.

Meoris sensed his mood and was quick to comfort him. "Of course you might visit Jochebed and her children again when your schedule permits."

She was careful not to make a definite promise. She would make sure he was kept too busy even to think of his former home. He had many things to learn—things that would crowd out the folk tales he must have been taught by his mother. She had heard that the Hebrews had only one God, and she supposed Jochebed would have mentioned Him to Moses.

Three days later, dressed in white linen and carefully coached by Meoris, Moses was presented to Rameses.

"Walk tall and bow low. Say as little as possible." Her instructions were simple enough, and Moses had mastered them. They walked together to Pharaoh's throne and bowed—very low.

Pharaoh commanded Moses to stand and looked intently at him for several silence-filled minutes. Moses returned his steady gaze.

A priest stepped forward and bowed to Rameses, then raised his head slightly to glare over at Moses, indicating strong disapproval of him. Rameses refused him permission to speak and waved him away with an impatient toss of his right hand.

Pharaoh would disregard the opinion of anyone else at such a time. He and he alone would decide about this boy. Moses had not moved his eyes since being commanded to stand for inspection; Pharaoh liked that. He liked everything he saw about this one his daughter had chosen to become a prince. A scribe stepped forward at Rameses' signal to present Moses' academic credentials. They were as favorable as Moses' appearance.

The Ruler of Upper and Lower Egypt, who occupied the incomparable Throne of Geb, god of the earth, stepped down from his platform, walked to where Moses stood and embraced him. Without a word he indicated his firm intent to place his beloved Egypt potentially in the hands of this one.

He clapped his hands sharply, signalling for Meoris to stand beside her young man. "You are to adopt him at once. He will have your claim to the Throne of Geb. You are responsible for his training. I will see him again in three years—not before. By then he must complete prescribed goals on time—and complete them extremely well!"

"As you say, he will do."

"Good. See to it."

_____11

Moses was educated in all the wisdom of the Egyptians and
was powerful in speech and action.   *Acts 7:22*

Moses was sent back to the school at On and was
assigned to Rahotep, a tutor with a wrinkled face and white
hair. He considered reading to be the skill basic to all other
fields of learning and was merciless in his assignments. He
deluged his young student with the poetry of Egypt and
with the practical maxims of Ptahotep. Moses found the poetry exciting but thought that it often was wasted on themes
of little importance, even absurdity. He enjoyed the maxims,
finding in many of them a beautifully phrased version of the
teachings he had received from Jochebed in his earlier
years—the value of wisdom and learning; the necessity of
discipline and well-defined goals; the physical and mental
benefits of a cheerful disposition.

Moses was also to master the writing of Egyptian hier-
oglyphics—a skill he was eager to perfect. And Rahotep insisted that he become familiar with the Akkadian language,
which was used for international commerce in Egypt, Canaan and Mesopotamia.

His versatile teacher introduced Moses to higher mathematics and taught him the geography and history of Egypt.
During a history lesson Moses once asked Rahotep about
something his mother had related to him—the invasion and
reign of the Hyksos people. The old scholar raised his head
high and said, "I did not hear you. *But,* if you repeat that
question—*ever*—I *will* hear you. I promise you!"

Rahotep was foremost in the group of priests who believed corporal punishment was a fundamental part of education, and Moses was given a liberal amount of it. An infraction of the rules, an inadequate response or a question considered to be impertinent—such as the one about the Hyksos—invited the stinging bite of the teacher's whip. Sometimes Moses felt imposed on—felt that many of the demands made on him were heavier than those made on any of the other boys. He didn't know if it was because more was required of a prince or because the priests did not approve of him. He sensed it was the latter but shrugged it off as something neither he nor they could do anything about. And when he remembered stories of the taskmasters over his people, he was embarrassed to complain about strict teachers.

Moses' favorite class was writing—from the first day he was given a clay tablet and stylus. He practiced and practiced, kneading the clay to erase when he wanted to write some more. He was eager to begin learning the principles of drafting to gain skill in executing the complicated and fascinating pictorial words and symbols of the Egyptian language.

His days of work were always as long as Miriam's and Aaron's—sometimes longer. After sundown he still mined the treasure of knowledge for himself and for his people. Many times, even after going to bed, he would lie awake trying to cipher a problem or remember an elusive hieroglyph. He was always awakened in time to be in his classroom by sunrise.

In rare moments when he could have idle thoughts, he sometimes wondered whether what was happening could be real or just a dream. Was he actually being groomed to become a person of authority in Mizraim—Egypt? If he ever did receive authority, he had no doubt what his first official action would be. He would free the captive Hebrews and allow them to go back to their God-given homeland. That was his motivation to excel—not fear of his teachers or a desire to please Meoris, not even a drive to become the next

Pharaoh—except as these were necessary steps toward freeing his people.

After his second year of study, he was given a week's vacation and went by royal chariot back to Meoris at the palace. She had planned entertainment for him on an extravagant scale. There would be banquets with the best food, the choicest wine and the most beautiful dancing girls. There would be wrestling matches and duels and a hunting trip into the desert for panthers, lions and pythons, which lived near the occasional water holes.

Moses, demonstrating that he had learned to assume authority, said he would attend none of these things until he had been allowed to visit his family.

Meoris was visibly disappointed but arranged for him to take the short journey to the cottage on Rekhmire's estate. She thought it was dangerous for Moses to do it, and she was unhappy about the place his family still held in his affections.

"You may stay one hour." She doubted that one hour could do much harm.

Now it was Moses' turn to be disappointed. Only an hour! He would have to say a lot in that hour; his family would, too.

Miriam wanted to know if Moses ate from dishes cut from alabaster or on plates of silver and gold. Aaron asked if he had hunted ibex, gazelle or lion.

He told Miriam he had seen elegant dinnerware once or twice but was away at school most of the time. There he ate from pottery similar to that in their mother's kitchen. He told Aaron he had no time for hunting.

Jochebed asked if he had studied any of the magic arts of Egypt and if he took part in any of the ritual processions to honor Egyptian gods and goddesses.

It was time to assume authority again. "If you keep asking so many questions, I won't get to tell you of the exciting things I have seen and learned—or of how I want it to work for the good of our people."

He began by talking of some of the least exciting things, saving the best part until last. He described the backless bench he sat on all day at school and of working late into the night by inadequate lamplight. He told of the high standards he was expected to meet, of the prejudice of the priests and of the whips—and that he often felt he was in bondage, too.

Miriam and Aaron were silent. Moses read in their eyes and attitudes a quick outrage when he mentioned he was in bondage. If even his hardships made them jealous, he hesitated to go on to share his accomplishments, wanting to spare them additional resentment. When he stopped talking, neither his sister nor his brother had any questions or comments.

Jochebed understood his problems but knew he had the stamina and motivation to overcome them. She expressed no approval or disapproval of anything he had said, but since her time with him was so short, she turned the conversation in a different direction.

"Moses, the Lord God has given you a sharp mind and the opportunity to fill it with wisdom and knowledge. Remember . . . wisdom comes from the Lord God; knowledge you can get from your teachers and from experience.

"Live as God directs you; listen for His voice. Your future is not tied to Mizraim. You are a descendant of Abraham; you are of the nation of Israel, tribe of Levi, house of Gershom. Your land is Canaan. There is no greater heritage than that of the children of Abraham—no greater future than ours.

"Pharaoh is a come-lately person whose gods are the sun, a frog, a river . . . and himself!"

Moses looked in open admiration at the beloved woman whose speech had brought tears to her eyes and to his. This woman, who had known nothing but slavery, claimed a heritage and a future greater than that of the ruler of Egypt!

Moses' attendant signaled it was time to return to the palace. Moses nodded, embraced his mother, said his goodbye to his sister and brother and walked to his chariot, calling over his shoulder, "I'll remember!"

As he was driven back to the palace, he thought of each word his mother had said; he pondered the Source of her hope and faith.

He also thought of the loss of communication between himself and his family, the lack of understanding between him and his brother and sister. He wished it were not so, even as he realized the gulf between them would widen in the years ahead.

He sighed, then gradually smiled as he turned his thoughts to banquets, dancing girls and the big game hunt. Meoris was thoughtful. He looked at the large sapphire ring on his right hand, a reminder that Meoris was also generous.

She was watching for him to return. "Did you see Jochebed, Miriam and Aaron?"

"Yes."

"Are they well?"

"Yes."

"Moses, I give you my word that they will be well cared for; you are not to be concerned about them. Your full attention is to be on your studies.

"When you go back to school this time your classes will be accelerated and will include additional ones; you will be studying law, and you are to be initiated into the mysteries of our religion, which have been secretly preserved in our temples and passed along to worthy ones from generation to generation. Some of our occult sciences came from priests in ancient Mesopotamia, and this knowledge is power."

Moses went to his room to rest and to think about the day. His reunion with his family was unsatisfying. They were becoming strangers. Meoris said his studies would get more complicated and would include learning things his mother had especially warned him against. He felt uneasy— as though he would be traitor to Jochebed if he went on with it and traitor to Meoris if he didn't. One day, as his mother had said, he would have to decide between being Egyptian or Hebrew. Meanwhile—he would sleep.

Meoris went to her quarters, also to rest and to think about the day. She reinforced her intent to get Moses to forget his family and their teachings as quickly as possible.

The priests already were prejudiced against him, and she did not underestimate their power. Moses must try to please them and not insist on worshiping a God they did not recognize. Egypt had enough gods. At least one of them should suit Moses.

When Moses went back to On, he took with him the decision to become proficient as a scribe. This skill could open many doors; he might be chosen to transmit royal commands direct from Pharaoh to messengers or to keep records on men and material for the army or to transcribe facts and figures for Pharaoh's architects. Many scribes had access to information on the inner workings of government. Ability as a scribe also would enhance his opportunity to use the legal training Meoris ordered him to acquire.

Meoris had agreed. Rameses had been persuaded to demand it. The tutors at On complied. Moses would be a scribe.

He was given a rectangular wooden pallet with two depressions in it for ink—one for red, one for black. His pens fit in a center groove on the pallet. Other supplies were a shell water pot and a linen rag for an eraser. He found it simpler to erase with a swipe of his tongue.

Moses mixed water with soot for the black ink and worked red ochre and water together for red ink. He was taught to prepare his pen from rushes by pounding them at one end to make a fine brush. He found it quicker to disregard the proper technique and simply to chew the ends of the rushes.

Processing papyrus stalks was complicated and time-consuming; the work usually was divided among different groups of workers. Some went to where the papyrus grew and cut the stalks just above the water level, then sliced it into convenient lengths and pared away the outer layer. Another group took the pithy part that was left and cut it into thin strips to lay on linen sheets with each strip overlapping another horizontally. Then other strips were laid on top, overlapping vertically. And after all that came the most monotonous part, which Moses tried to avoid whenever possible—the papyrus strips had to be pounded with a wooden mallet for an hour and a half. The juice that was worked out of the papyrus was perfect for holding the strips together. The final step was to burnish the sheet with a stone.

Once the students mastered all steps of the procedure, servants did the work for them so they could spend more time in studying astronomy or geometry or any of a dozen other arts and sciences.

Moses found it difficult to take the study of the Egyptian gods and goddesses seriously, especially the more ridiculous ones such as Bes, the dwarfish god who wore a leopard skin and an elaborate ostrich headdress, and Bastet, the goddess with the head of a cat, and Hathor with her cow's head. His mind reeled with the names and imputed accomplishments of the deities:

Osiris, judge of the dead

Re-harakhte, Amon-re and Aton—three sun gods

Atum, the creator god

Horus, the hawk-headed sky god, whose one eye is the sun and the other the moon

Montu, the god of war

The family of Amon, god of war and wind—his wife, Mut, and his son, Khonsu

The children of Osiris—Isis, Set and Nephthys

Wadjet, goddess of Lower Egypt

Nekhbet, goddess of Upper Egypt

Seshet, goddess of learning

Anybis, the jackal-headed god of cemeteries and embalming rites

Sobek, the crocodile god

Toth, who invented numbers

Kephra, Buto, Neith, Min—and still more!

To Moses, studying these myriad gods and goddesses was confusing and senseless. But there was a fascination in the temple rituals and in the grand processions and festivals. He intended to keep the line between interest in them and worship of them clear in his mind.

The more he thought about these deities and the more he learned of the implausible superstitions surrounding them, the more he treasured the sublime simplicity of Jochebed's teaching when she spoke in hushed tones of the one God, who was called by several names, each of them describing a facet of His being, all of them calling up thoughts of beauty and holiness.

With so great a God as the Hebrews had, they should build Him a temple more elaborate than anything Egypt ever dared to try. But He had only rough stone altars here and there around Goshen and a few similar ones said to have been left in Canaan by Abraham, Isaac and Jacob-Israel.

Some day, Moses thought, I would like to build a temple for the one God. When I am in a place of power, just as soon as I let the Hebrew people go free, that will be my next project.

And as the years went by, Moses became well educated in all the arts and sciences of Egypt.

12

The Egyptian oracles counseled the king to make use of Moses in the war with the Ethiopians, and the Egyptians made him general of their army.

Josephus Antiquities of the Jews 2. 10. 1.

In his late twenties Moses exchanged the school room for the practical arena. His first occupation was as an official scribe handling diplomatic exchanges between Egypt and its buffer states to the east. Written in the international Akkadian language, correspondence between Pharaoh's court and the vassal princelings of Canaan was active enough to provide an interesting challenge.

It was Rameses—after subtle hints from his priestly advisers—who decided Moses' education was incomplete. Meoris had not seen to it that he received sufficient military training.

He was recalled from his diplomatic work and placed in the ranks of foot soldiers. In a series of quick promotions he was given rank equal to Khamus. Commander Khamus, priding himself in his years of capable leadership and in the wealth of military experience he had amassed, resented Moses—not only because of his rapid promotions but also because his unique ability warranted them.

Khamus used his influence with Rameses to persuade him to honor Moses' request to be returned to civilian life as soon as possible. He was allowed to return to the work of a scribe, but Rameses decided he should work next at On as a temple scribe. Moses continued to feel he was merely a royal slave moved from one place to another, but his title was impressive: Chief Scribe. He copied portions of Egypt's sacred archives. The priests resented him even more because they rightly felt that the chief scribe was not properly impressed by the words he was copying.

Moses was concerned that in the nearly 10 years since he began his professional career he had alienated many men—both in the military and in the priesthood. But he believed his claim to Pharaoh's throne had become unquestioned in spite of their opposition. Meoris had told him that neither Emwise nor Kha was being considered any longer as contenders for the throne, and Merneptah's chances were next to nothing. Rameses had been impressed with Moses' brief military career.

Now legions of Ethiopians threatened Egypt's southern border. Egypt, taken by surprise, was thrust into a defensive war. A distraught Rameses sought advice from his oracles and was told to put Moses in charge of the army immediately.

Pharaoh issued the orders, and once more Moses obeyed. The young commander felt certain this assignment was not due to a request from Khamus; he believed the priests of On had devised this means of permanently disposing of him by sending him to the front line.

Moses studied the situation he faced and talked with soldiers who knew the terrain of that border area. Then he planned his attack and ordered supplies.

Meoris was one of the many who watched Egypt's legions leave for the south with Moses leading. Marching men with scarlet and gold banners surrounded his gleaming chariot. An elite contingent behind the chariot carried a caged falcon, which was the army's talisman symbol of the golden god, Horus, who was personified by Rameses the Great. The parade of military strength proceeded—soldiers with shining lances, spears and shields and freshly scrubbed war chariots manned by expert horsemen and bowmen. Last of all was a corps of soldiers with unusual gear—70 caged ibis. Moses had ordered these heronlike birds to overcome a formidable enemy his men would encounter before they engaged the Ethiopian army—poisonous serpents! In order to take his foe by surprise, Moses' strategy included crossing a swampy area where the ibis would dart at the snakes and snap them into their long, slender, curved bills.

The army moved quickly southward, but when the swamp area was reached, the advance was slowed considerably as war chariots, no longer polished and shiny, became mired in mud and had to be pushed along by sweating foot soldiers. But they did not have to worry about snakes; the freed ibis soon found their prey.

The surprise attack was launched from a direction the Ethiopian army least expected. The Egyptians surged against the enemy, forcing them back from the border area. Moses led his men in close pursuit into the Ethiopian countryside, and the civilians joined the military forces in retreat.

They fled to the impregnable island city of Saba. It towered above the wide, crocodile-infested river that surrounded it. Even if Moses could have secured makeshift boats, the land across the river was too steep and smooth to climb. The refugees had scrambled to safety up ladders, then pulled the ladders up after them. They were safe.

Moses laid siege. The food supply in Saba was inadequate for more than a few weeks because of the number of people who had swarmed to it. Rations were sparingly doled out, but administrators were in panic and pleaded with their monarch to make peace with the Egyptians.

Moses received the royal messenger and a settlement was negotiated. He would return to Rameses in a fraction of the time Khamus had estimated it would take. The priests would be disappointed that he returned at all.

The Egyptian border was safe again, and Moses had many barges filled with the spoils of the brief war:

500 Nubian slaves

100 elephant tusks

12 each of leopards, panthers and apes

7 bales of ostrich feathers

5 bags of carefully guarded gold nuggets

The Nile's current carried them northward, and wherever its flow slackened even slightly, oarsmen were put into duty. Everyone was eager to return with the good news and the tangible tokens of victory.

Moses staged a procession from the river up the main road to the palace. Everyone for miles in all directions turned out to watch the hero come home from war.

Meoris, the princess, was proud because her protege was the pride of their whole country. Meoris, the adoptive mother, was thankful her son was home safely.

And Meoris, the politician, gave a banquet in Moses' honor. She invited Khamus, the priests, the great wives—and Emwise, Kha and Merneptah—and hundreds of others. No one refused an invitation such as this, and all who came understood they would join in celebrating Moses' victory—and would be expected to toast the hero. Meoris planned the banquet to be the most lavish one in anyone's memory; she planned the entertainment to be dazzling. This was her victory, too!

Meoris was escorted into the banquet hall by her son. He was dressed in white linen, the short skirt perfectly pleated. He wore a wide collar of gold and seven finger rings of agate, carnelian, lapis lazuli and different shades of sapphire.

Meoris was elegant in pale blue sheer linen. Her gown was draped over one shoulder, leaving the other shoulder bare; its soft folds flattered her slender figure. She also wore a golden collar, fit for a princess—set with white jasper and topaz. She had used mascara to match her gown and a flattering coral color for her lip rouge. Her black hair glistened with pomade and hung long and straight from under a golden headband. Blue linen and papyrus sandals revealed well-tended nails colored with henna.

Dinner included Meoris's favorite foods—dates steeped in sweet wine, tender gazelle, and fresh bounty from Egypt's gardens and orchards. There was a sumptuous variety of breads and cheeses and plentiful fish. The cooks and bakers had surpassed everyone's expectations.

Stewards kept golden wine goblets filled. Musicians and dancers entertained during the feast. Later there were wrestlers, acrobats, magicians and more dancing girls. Pharaoh presented Moses with a dagger with a carved ivory handle.

The festivities went on for hours. Being a hero was demanding, but especially for Meoris's sake the commander decided to play his part well—and he found it enjoyable.

When the evening finally was over and he was in his own quarters on a cushioned couch, his mind reeled from all he had experienced in those preceding hours and in the exhausting weeks of the intense campaign in Ethiopia. He felt engulfed—overwhelmed. It was just too much—too much!

He closed his eyes and suddenly remembered—for no seemingly coherent reason—sitting with Aaron one rare evening when his brother had time to relax. They finished a supper of bread, fish, lentils and dates and then played a game of checkers; it had seemed like a wondrous celebration. Bread . . . and fish . . . and a game of checkers . . .

Just before sleep came he thought of how he had increased the riches of Egypt by his courage and skill, even though his longing still was to help his own people. His victory seemed hollow, the regal celebration shallow.

The banquet was only the beginning of the gala treatment of Egypt's most handsome, heroic general. He was taken on a lavish ceremonial barge on the Nile. The trip officially began at On with the traditional ceremony of the blessing of the priests. It continued south to Memphis, passing pyramids and temples that were built to be seen to best advantage from the river, on to Beni Hasan and Akhetaton. It was a restful time except when the crew tied the barge up for the night along the shore. Crowds of noisy people, alerted to the approach of Pharaoh's barge, tried to get a glimpse of Moses. Their loud din was stopped only when louder shouts of Moses' guards demanded quiet.

With a favorable current and the machinelike rowing of the oarsmen, they proceeded to Thebes where the grand Ramesseum still was being built. Moses was taken on an inspection tour of the site. He walked past its 134 towering columns on the facade and into the pillared halls of the shrine that was hollowed out of the rock. Four statues of

Rameses, each 60 feet high, would be dragged to this location soon.

On the east bank of the Nile were the Karnak and Luxor temples, each one an immense combination of gold, silver, jewels, mosaic work, stone carvings, brilliant tiles and paintings. They were ostentatious, extravagant and intricately detailed—grand beyond words.

Returning to the Ramesseum site before leaving the area, Moses was more aware of the slaves than of the building under way. Hundreds and hundreds of slaves, doing what often was literally backbreaking work, swarmed over the location like ants, with the temples as their awesome anthills. The work was behind schedule, so the cracking whips of the overseers bit many more bare backs and legs than usual, and the number of daily working hours was increased. Slaves who died under the merciless requirements were considered fortunate by many who lived to face another and another and another day.

The original plan was for the barge to go as far south as Abu Simbel, and for Moses this was to be the exciting climax of the trip. Since the last word his mother had about his father was that he was being sent there, Moses was determined, if possible, to find out if he were alive or at least to find someone who knew him and could tell something about him. But as the boat was being readied for departure from Thebes, an aide rushed to Moses with a small scroll.

He bowed low and said, "Exalted General of the forces of the Golden Horus, I bring a message to you."

"Unless it is very important I will accept it later, after we are on our way."

"It is from Pharaoh's own hand, delivered by his messengers in his own chariot. They have driven night and day."

Moses took the scroll and read his latest instructions. He was to go no further south. There was a rumor of a serious slave uprising about to begin at Abu Simbel, and Moses was not to be involved in it. General Khamus would attend to it.

And Moses, who had commanded a victorious army, now at Pharaoh's word meekly ordered the barge to be turned around and headed north. It would go with the current—even as he himself would.

But as he obeyed Pharaoh, he thought of the father he had never known except as he lived in the stories his mother told. Moses hoped he was alive and part of the uprising and that he would be the winner of the quarrel with the taskmasters. Then he shrugged his shoulders at the fantasy of those thoughts. Surely his father had been dead for many years, and slaves had no chance of winning a quarrel. Each bloody revolt ended in torture for the instigators, and the fate of slaves everywhere was made more unbearable by Mizraim's reprisals. Mizraim! He hadn't used that name for Egypt for a long time.

Back in Egypt's capital, Moses spent less time thinking of the marvels of the Ramesseum and the temples at Karnak and Luxor than he did of those antlike workers—and of the brave, foolish rebels at Abu Simbel.

He had postponed for far too long a visit with his mother, brother and sister. He went to Pharaoh to ask for a leave of absence—from the army, from the court, from everything.

"Go! Stay as long as you are pleased to stay—anywhere you wish. Do not let your military success and the praises of the people cause you to feel indispensable to Rameses the Great!"

His words were measured and implied a warning. The mighty ruler of Upper and Lower Egypt remembered his own years of military victories and the adulation of his people and saw in Moses' current triumph something he never could experience again. Moses already was his successor in the hearts of the Egyptians. And Pharaoh was displeased.

—*13*

He chose to be mistreated along with the people of God rather than to enjoy the pleasures of sin for a short time.

Hebrews 11:25

Moses expected to find changes on the Rekhmire estate, but he had not imagined the changes would be so dramatic.

Aaron was not there. He had managed to get transferred to a stonecutting crew and was working at Akhetaton. He seldom got back to see Miriam and his mother; he had married a lovely girl named Elisheba and had one child, Nadab.

Miriam was married to Hur of the tribe of Levi. Hur was a large, likable man. He had a responsible position in charge of Rekhmire's stable of horses. Miriam's work-roughened hands and weathered face were eloquent testimony of her years of working in the gardens and fields. She had grown to look more like her mother—as Moses remembered his mother.

Jochebed now was stooped and white-haired, but still vibrant, loving—and lovable. The moment she saw him she got up from the bench where she had been passing the morning hours slowly weaving straw into a small mat. She stood, reaching out her arms toward her son.

Moses ran to her, caught her up in his arms as easily as she had once lifted him so many years before. They embraced, then gently pushed apart to see each other better.

She looked long at the prince—and was pleased to see he was still her strong, lively son.

He looked at his mother and saw in her eyes the suffering of his people, saw in her smile their courage and heard in her voice the hope of a people straining for freedom.

They talked for the rest of the day, scarcely taking time to eat and even then talking between bites. Moses wanted to know about her, about Aaron and his family, about Miriam and her husband. Jochebed wanted to hear about the world beyond Goshen, the world she could not imagine—the world Moses was helping to shape.

In the late evening Miriam and Hur joined them, and Moses gave presents to his family—turquoise necklaces for his mother and sister, a senit board for Hur, and two fine linen tunics for each of them.

The next day he and his mother sat on the bench by her front door. The burst of excitement of the previous day had waned, and Moses didn't recount any more of his accomplishments, although there were many he hadn't shared.

"Are you quiet today because you think my mind can't hold any more of your stories? You may be right. In that case, just tell me over again all you said yesterday, and then when it's impressed on my mind, you can tell me more."

"I'm quiet because . . . reciting things I've done and things I've learned doesn't give me much satisfaction or pleasure. I'm unsettled, unfulfilled . . . as though I should be doing something else. Why? Why is it like this?"

"You have no idea why, Moses?"

"I have an idea."

"And that is . . . ?"

"It is . . . that I have to decide if I am to be Egyptian or Hebrew."

Jochebed reached over and patted his arm the way she had done when he was a young boy. Her eyes were smiling, and her time-lined face was smiling, too. "I believe the Lord God has controlled and guided everything that has happened to you. I believe He is also giving you this dissatisfaction instead of pride, because all of what has been up until now is only preparation for what you will yet do."

"Do you think I can do greater things than lead a victorious Egyptian army? Do you think I ever again will learn as much as I've learned in these past years?"

"I think . . . I think you will scarcely be remembered for what you've done so far."

Moses was amused at Jochebed's dismissal of his exploits. "My mother, if it takes more than all I've done so far to be remembered, then I am content to be forgotten. But . . . just what would you think I'd have to do . . . to be remembered in future times?"

Jochebed didn't answer. She just smiled a little and nodded her head as if she were sharing a secret with herself.

Moses' laughter had died away, and he became very serious. "You've always thought I'd be the Lord God's choice to lead our people back to Canaan . . ."

"Both your father and I believed this almost from the moment you were born. But this does not make it so. It will be so only if the Lord God calls you Himself."

"You used to tell me how He talked to Abraham, to Isaac and to Jacob. But He hasn't spoken to anyone since then. Why do you think He ever will?"

She didn't answer his question but pursued her own line of thought. "Doesn't it seem that the unique things that have happened to you are evidence of the hand of El Shaddai?"

"Yes . . . yes . . . but He has not spoken."

This time she did not evade. "He speaks to His servants when they are listening, waiting on Him. Perhaps, Moses, you have been too busy learning, working, leading armies and practicing the politics of the court."

"Perhaps."

"You have told me of wonderfully grand temples to the gods and kings of Mizraim, but do you have an altar where you worship the Lord God?"

"No."

"Why not?"

The Egyptian prince was finding it difficult to answer, but he made an attempt. "I've been . . . as you said . . . busy. Busy answering thousands of demands, driven to learn, to think, to analyze, to direct, to go to war, to write, to plan, to . . . to go to banquets. Pressures and goals, goals and pressures!"

His mother just smiled; she had another question. "Do you see why Abraham was called out of the great city of Ur of the Chaldees?"

Moses was quiet, so she phrased the question another way. "Do you understand why Jacob met the Lord God when he was alone at Bethel—and again at a lonely sentry post at Peniel?"

Of course he understood—but he wasn't Abraham, and he wasn't Jacob, and he had many things to handle. His problem was getting his mother to understand. He wanted to change the subject, but she kept talking.

"Moses, wait on the Lord God. Seek His guidance in all things. Don't run ahead of His timing. Learn to wait before Him in reverent worship and adoration. Pray through the night and on through the day when you are striving toward a decision."

"If I must take time to wait quietly for the Lord God to speak to me . . . if it takes hours, night into day . . . then I may never hear Him. Except for this time with you these two days, it seems I've had no respite in the many years since I moved away from here. My days are totally planned for me, and I'm trained to respond 'quickly and well'!"

"If the Lord God wills you to listen to Him, and yet you don't make a time to listen to Him . . . He can overrule your circumstances to provide the necessary quiet, as He did for His servants in time past.

"His voice! Moses! What would it be worth to you to hear His voice?"

"Everything I own!"

"What would it be worth to you . . . to be His person of special concern?"

"The riches of Egypt!"

That night as Jochebed prayed to the Lord God, she thanked Him for all the marvelous blessings He had showered on her son. Most especially she thanked Him for keeping Moses unsettled and dissatisfied in the midst of triumph and plenty—for giving him a persistent longing for divine direction from the God of Abraham, Isaac, and Jacob.

Then, as she had entrusted her baby to the Lord God 40 years before, she now entrusted this dearly, dearly beloved prince.

In another part of the cottage the prince was unable to sleep. Who was he? The next Pharaoh of Egypt? Hero of the land? Or a Hebrew like the other Hebrews, waiting for his God's guidance—longing for a tangible sign of His presence? Moses' homecoming was to have been a peaceful respite; it was becoming a spiritual struggle.

Moses had planned to spend a longer time with his family, but he became more restless and decided he couldn't spend day after day talking of the past and conjecturing about the future. He would come back to visit again before his month's leave was over, but first he would try to find Aaron—perhaps even his father. He told Jochebed he would leave the next morning.

Moses had grown accustomed to feeling that every place he set his foot in Egypt was his, or practically so. Meoris encouraged him to expect to be Rameses' successor, probably even installed as coregent before the aging ruler died. The envy of the sons of the great wives and the enmity of the priests and high-ranking military officers had seemed a threat for a while, but now with his dazzling victory and his great rapport with the people, his ascending the Throne of Geb should be a natural course of events. He still had strong backing from some of the military men and from a few of the sacred scribes; more important, he had the benefit of Meoris's understanding of court politics, and he had his own skills and daring and ambition.

Such were his thoughts as he rode with his driver and aide in his royal chariot toward Akhetaton. He supposed he should take this time and use it "waiting before the Lord" as his mother had suggested, but he had so much thinking to do! He had to plan this meeting with Aaron. Should he mention the imminent possibility of his becoming Pharaoh, or at least coregent? Would that make Aaron glad—or resentful?

Then, as his mother often did, he "thought-talked" to help firm up his plans and ideas. "My first official decree will be unpopular with the Egyptians. It will upset the economy and accelerate the Egyptians' hostility against my own people. Nevertheless, I will do it. I will give the Hebrews their freedom. I will allow them to go to Canaan. I will be great in history for this. I will be ranked with Abraham, Isaac, Jacob and Joseph. I'll be the most famous. Egypt would not dare erase my name from their records as they did those names of the Shepherd Kings, Apophis and Salitis. And even if they did, my people would remember my name wherever they are, as they remembered the names of the Hyksos and taught them to their children. The Hebrews have a talent for record keeping and remembering!"

He wanted his meeting with Aaron to be without fanfare, so as he neared Akhetaton he dismissed his chariot driver and personal guard and sent them back to Rameses. He put on the unfamiliar clothes of a peasant and walked out to mingle with the slaves. He no longer wore white linen, the gold collar or the impressive jewelry. His clothing was simply a coarse, short skirt. Bare from the waist up, no sandals on his feet, he walked among his brothers.

In his familiar Egyptian world of palaces, schools, temples, diplomatic circles, and military conquests he never forgot that his people were being crushed in the dehumanizing cruelty of slavery. He knew it, but he had not looked, as now he did, at what those words meant. The gaunt frames, staring eyes and mechanical movements of aching muscles tugging at a rope to move a mass of stone—or lifting brick after brick without respite until the day was ended—defined "dehumanizing." The crack of the long leather whip and the shriek it evoked as the victim fell bleeding in the dust demonstrated "cruelty."

He had been unable to locate Aaron and no longer wanted to face him. He could not cope even to think of his elder brother being beaten down like these slaves among whom he walked. If Aaron had only stayed at the estate, Meoris's protection would have continued to help him have an easier life. Why had he chosen to leave? What had he experienced since then? Was he alive? Which would be better for Aaron—life as these slaves lived it or death?

Suppose he did meet his brother. How would the knowledge he had mined for his people help lift Aaron's load? How could the promise of a throne ease Aaron's bitter existence as a slave?

The tormenting questions for which he had no answers were making his head throb. Then in one crashing second Moses felt hot, searing pain across his back. Before he could catch his breath another sharp sting bit into his flesh. This time the whip wound around his legs and he fell. He was roughly shoved over onto his bleeding back, and with a guard's sturdy sandal on his neck and a spear menacing his chest, he dared not struggle.

An arrogant voice was demanding information. "Whose work crew are you with?"

With the pressure of the sandaled foot still on his throat, he could barely reply. "No one's . . . crew . . . I . . . alone."

"Then I need papers showing that you are allowed near this temple site while construction is going on." The foot was withdrawn, and the spear, still firmly grasped, was pushed into the sandy ground.

Moses felt the luxury of being able to swallow, of taking a deep breath. He raised himself up slightly and leaned on one elbow. He almost could hear Meoris's haughty voice telling him over and over, "Assume authority." In pain, in danger, in humiliation—Moses laughed softly as he thought of that advice. He would try. Could Pharaoh's great general command even one overseer without his royal insignia and armed men?

The whip slashed his shoulder and sent him falling on his back again. "You dare laugh, stupid one?" The guard was unnerved and made his spear ready, convinced this man he had apprehended was mad!

"I . . . dare . . . laugh." Moses slowly sat up, then stood— a foot taller than the guard. He stared at the Egyptian with the same steady gaze he had given Pharaoh that day long ago when he stood before him for approval. The guard, unused to the strength transmitted through that unwavering eye contact, stepped back a pace or two.

With the resonance of a cultured voice and with an unmistakable air of one assuming authority, Moses continued. "I will tell you who I am, and then you will tell me who you are. I am Moses, general of Pharaoh's army, chief scribe of the glorious temple at On, master scribe of the eastern outposts. I am on leave from my official duties to test the zeal and wisdom of the overseers at Akhetaton. I can attest to your zeal, but not your wisdom."

He paused for a moment to allow the miserable guard to realize the implication of what he had said. Then quickly pulling from his waist the ivory-handled dagger, he brandished it as proof of who he was and as a threat that he would use it if necessary. "I am also the favorite of Pharaoh, who has given me this dagger.

"Now! Your name! Tell it correctly, for some in this crowd of gawkers we have attracted will, if you don't . . . and it will be the worse for you."

"Tmenuh, sir." The guard looked pale.

"Tmenuh, you are dismissed." Moses imitated Pharaoh's wide arm swing, which he used to denote gracious forbearance. Tmenuh walked away quickly and became busy at once, checking the work his men were doing. Only then did he realize that Moses had relieved him of his whip at some point during their confrontation.

"I'll take you to where you can have your wounds bathed in oil and where you can get a new tunic to cover the lash marks." A young lad, moved more by hope of a large reward than by compassion, volunteered to see to Moses' immediate needs.

"Good. I will follow you. Hurry!"

The gawkers dispersed, not really believing what they had seen.

The self-assured prince of Egypt became a confused, angry and impatient man. How dared Egypt do this! Who was Egypt? Was he?

Time lost meaning for him. He didn't know if he had been walking three hours or four or five since that shattering experience with Tmenuh. He thought of the little good he could do if he walked among the slaves for the rest of his life—or even worked alongside them. He became obsessed with the nothingness of who he was and with his power-lessness really to do anything about the abhorrent slavery that clearly was an attempt not just to subjugate but to elim-inate a people—his people!

14

Glancing this way and that and seeing no one, he killed the
Egyptian and hid him in the sand.   *Exodus 2:12*

Moses turned aside from the road and walked toward the river. He didn't want to see another slave or another taskmaster—not ever! If he couldn't change things,
why should he continue to put himself through the torment
of these last hours? He would find a quiet place to think—
away from the sight and the sound and the stench of bondage.

He heard a scuffling ahead, and with the practiced skill
of a military man, he moved to where he could determine
its exact source. A Hebrew slave, obviously trying to run
away, had been overtaken by his overseer. The Egyptian's
back was to Moses; he was holding the slave by the back of
his neck with one hand and pounding his face with the
other.

In one flashing moment that slave came to represent to
Moses all of the Hebrews—descendants of Abraham—sons
of Jacob—family. That slave, like Aaron, was his brother! At
the same time the guard came to represent the total Egyptian
oppression.

He could not free all the slaves, but he would avenge
one! He grasped the ivory handle of the ceremonial dagger.
Sunlight glanced on its blade as Moses lunged toward the
guard and made a swift, deadly thrust with his weapon.

Moses literally shook with emotions he couldn't fully de-
fine. He experienced energy-sapping waves of astonishment

at what he had done, fear of its consequences, remorse—and futility.

Then slowly, reluctantly, he forced himself to do the next necessary thing; he buried the Egyptian in the sand. The slave had disappeared. Moses, almost in shock, turned from the riverbank and made his way back to the road.

He had no idea how far he had walked when he came to a small grove of palm trees. He turned off the road and sat down, leaning against one of the trees, which both supported his back and hid him from the road. Evening was draping the landscape in shadows. Had it been only that morning when he had arrived in Akhetaton? The prince of Egypt could not believe that one day could have held so many shattering hours.

He closed his eyes. Weak from emotional and physical traumas but feeling that he must stay alert, he would be careful not to sleep.

In the semidarkness of early morning he arose and made his way to a nearby settlement. Slaves were already being ordered by brusque overseers armed with whips to begin the daily march to the construction site. He walked down a narrow dirt street, feeling more tired than ever before in his life.

A few yards ahead of him a fight was going on. From its intensity Moses thought an overseer was indulging in some rough persuasion. He quickened his steps; he would settle at least one more account with Mizraim. When he got closer to the men, he saw they were both Hebrews.

With his perfected "assumed authority" he raised his voice to stop the fight, asking the aggressor, "Why are you hitting your fellow Hebrew?"

The man let go of his opponent to turn menacingly on this stranger who had interfered in a personal matter. His eyes narrowed to scrutinize the unwelcome referee, then they widened in surprise. From rumors that had swept through their quarters the night before he realized he was facing a fugitive—a murderer running from Egyptian authorities, a dangerous man who might kill again! He tried to take the initiative to keep his cold fear from showing:

"Who made you ruler and judge over us?"

This slave had asked the question Moses was struggling with. Was he, indeed, to be ruler and judge in Egypt? Had the Lord God called him to that? The Lord God had never called at all! Would he then choose to be counted with the oppressor or with the oppressed?

Making the most of the advantage he seemed to have since this stranger had become mute, the slave continued with an accusing taunt: "Are you thinking of killing me as you killed the Egyptian?"

Again Moses didn't answer, but each word cut into his mind; each word broke his heart. He had alienated these two Hebrews by trying to be a peacemaker; he had lost track of another slave who had run off alone, probably to die or to be killed. His first attempts to be the champion of the Hebrews could not have been less productive. Moses, oriented to success and accomplishment, felt the sharp stab of failure and the sudden devastation of fear—fear for his very life.

He experienced a rapid sequence of thoughts, some logical, some intuitive—each one disturbing. If these men knew of the murder, which he had been certain was unobserved, the Egyptian authorities surely would know of it, too. A crime of this importance would be reported to higher and higher echelons. It would be only a matter of time until it came to the attention of one of Pharaoh's ministers who would piece together all the information and reach a certain conclusion. It would not be difficult; he had even given his name to that guard, Tmenuh!

He turned away from the quarreling slaves as though he had ceased to be aware of them.

His mind was filled with torrents of anxiety and despair. His enemies would exploit this situation. None of Pharaoh's scribes, ministers or priests knew for certain what his racial identity was, but some had concluded he was not Egyptian and once had hinted of this to Pharaoh. Rameses silenced them only by his anger, not by refuting their implications. Moses realized then that Rameses had surmised his actual origin; now his supposition would be confirmed. He would know beyond doubt where Moses' first allegiance was—and his rage would be fierce.

Beyond all this, Moses sensed that Pharaoh already was seeking an excuse to discredit him. His popularity and military success had aroused a thinly disguised jealousy. Moses was sure Pharaoh would be pleased if he had reason to imprison—or execute—one he had come to see as a rival for the worship of his people.

Moses stopped to buy bread at the next village. The storekeeper was talkative, glad for the chance to tell his news to another stranger. "There was a slave rebellion a few miles from here last night."

"What happened?"

"A slave got away and ran down to the riverbank. The guard of his labor gang caught up with him, but he was killed—stabbed!—then just covered over with sand . . . and the slave got away."

"They didn't catch him?"

"No, not yet. But they will find him—and maybe his helper. There were two men against that guard. They say the second man has been identified as a top Egyptian officer by someone who saw it all. It seems they were together in the army in Ethiopia, so he recognized the man but was too surprised to go after him until it was too late. So the Egyptian officer got away too, so far.

"And that's not all . . ." The man paused for dramatic effect, consciously enjoying the attention his customer was giving his story.

Moses, at a total loss for words, simply waited and hoped his reactions were not registering in his face.

After clearing his throat and leaning toward Moses, the merchant continued: "What do you think of this? An o-verseer in Akhetaton said he dealt with a troublemaker there early yesterday morning . . . and that one gave his name as Moses . . . of Pharaoh's household! There are those who say Moses was the Egyptian officer who killed the guard."

Moses forced a smile. "Do you always have tall stories to entertain your patrons?"

"Sometimes I tell yarns. But I never made up one this

big! Don't think it's true, myself. There's a lot of unrest among the slaves, and they invent stories just to stir up people . . . like this one about an Egyptian officer in disguise, calling himself Moses, killing an overseer just to defend a filthy slave." He shook his head as if to deny credence to the story he had just repeated.

Moses paid for his provisions and walked out of the shop, calling over his shoulder, "I'll stop in when I'm back this way. I want to find out how that story ends."

And how would the story end? How much time did he have before his name would be on the lips of search parties throughout Mizraim? He set out for Rekhmire's estate as fast as he could. It was dangerous, but he wanted to see Jochebed before he left the Nile country.

And then where would he go? Every road leading out of Mizraim would be watched. He would have to escape into the vast expanse of the desert to be safe for a while—until he could decide where to go for sanctuary.

As he walked, he tried to think and to plan. Canaan? Haran or Babylon? Midian or Damascus? Where? None of his ideas seemed feasible, and he was in a hurry. There was no time to pray!

15

Moses fled from Pharaoh and went to live in Midian.

Exodus 2:15

He arrived at Rekhmire's estate at midmorning. It had been a difficult trip—avoiding the highway, traveling most of the way by night, risking being taken as a thief instead of a murderer in hiding. Miriam was sitting near her cottage grinding grain. She saw him before he spoke.

"Moses! You look half dead. What happened? Wait— don't tell me now. Come into our house, and I'll bathe your feet. Then you can rest while I fix you something to eat . . . and then you can tell me what happened."

No scented bath at the palace was ever more refreshing than the basin of cool water Miriam brought to him. After he rested briefly, she brought fruit, cheese, bread and wine. He thanked her and ate in silence.

As she cleared away the lunch, she asked, "May I ask you one question?"

"Yes."

"Did you see Aaron?"

"No. But I saw my other brothers."

Moses' eyes were filled with tears and heavy from lack of sleep. Miriam motioned to a reed mat in the corner, and Moses lay down on it to sleep until late afternoon.

By the time he awoke, Hur had come in from the stables. Moses told both Miriam and her husband what had happened, why he was afraid, and what he planned to do. He didn't attempt to explain any of the frustration he felt with himself at his mishandling of things. He didn't try to communicate his despair at the sudden loss of everything he had worked toward for so long.

They didn't add to his burden by suggesting that along with the end of his personal hopes went the hope they and many others had of soon being freed from slavery by a powerful kinsman with decision-making power in Mizraim.

When he had finished speaking, Miriam simply said, "I'll go tell our mother . . . at least as much as she has to know."

"Tell her everything. And tell her she was right in saying I would have to decide one day to be either Egyptian or Hebrew. Tell her . . . I'm finished being an Egyptian . . . but since I have no way now to help my Hebrew people, she should give up her grand hopes for me. The Lord God must have chosen another to be the leader of His people.

"She taught us well, Miriam, but she was not always right in her judgments . . . certainly not in the one about my having a God-appointed mission. I'm . . . sorry . . . to disappoint her."

Miriam looked at him for a long time. She no longer saw a proud, confident prince; she felt again like an older sister watching over a helpless younger brother.

"I'll go to Mother now while you get ready for your journey. Go to the main kitchen; they will give you provisions. They won't have heard the news yet, so tell them we are going to have a celebration for you and we want any extra food they can spare.

"And . . . you will stop to say good-bye to our mother?"

"Yes. Tell her it will be for only a moment . . . no time for conversation."

"She will understand."

Moses walked to the building that housed the kitchen, a place familiar to him since he was a young child. It had the same pungent odor of yeast, the same sweltering heat around the ovens, the same baskets of fresh vegetables and fruit. He secured his necessary provisions without any difficulty. Rekhmire's slaves had been trained for years to oblige Moses, and since his recent success they were more eager than ever to indulge him.

Back at Miriam's cottage he stowed most of the food in his pack and added a few personal belongings; he was ready.

He walked to his mother's house; it was obvious Miriam had been there. Jochebed was sitting on a low stool. Her right hand lay in unaccustomed idleness in her lap. The rough fingertips of her left hand slowly traced and retraced her jawline. Occasionally she extended her forefinger across a wrinkled cheek to dab at her eyes.

She had been trying to come to terms with new, stern realities. Moses was going away—running from a crime—running for his life. She was used to his being gone, but this time it was different. This time he was not going to some school Meoris had selected for him, nor was he off on a special assignment for Pharaoh. This time she didn't know where he would go and didn't think he would be back—at least not in time to tell her of the world he found beyond Egypt. She allowed herself the rare indulgence of a few tears.

She found some consolation in remembering the early years she had spent with him. He had been educated by the wisest teachers in Egypt, but she had been his first teacher— his most devoted teacher. He would remember the heritage she had given him.

Her loving work had been accomplished with a definite sense of purpose, with a sense of perspective—and most of all, with the enabling power of El Shaddai! She managed a smile at that point. El Shaddai! Of course! Her work might be ended, but His was not! He would still use her son to set his people free. She had believed that too long to give up hope now.

"*Remember!*" Jochebed poured a lifetime of longing and striving and hoping into that word. Then tenderly, almost inaudibly, she added the old words: "Don't . . . forget." She was speaking to a prince who stood in her doorway.

Only with his eyes did he answer, "I will remember." Only with a nod of his head did he promise not to forget.

He walked across the narrow room to her and held her close. Then he turned to hurry from her sight. He felt weighted down with things he would remember, and he chafed under things he never could forget.

He started across familiar fields with long strides, clenching his fists in outrage at the world and at himself. There was no time to amend anything; he needed each moment just to run! Run—to where he knew no one, was known by no one! Run—into desolate desert wilderness.

He had been taught to equate waste with sin, and now waste seemed to be the symbol of his life. A knowledge of Egyptian arts and sciences was wasted on a desert fugitive; military strategy, logic and philosophy were incongruous with this monotonous trek across indefinite miles to an undefined goal. Even his learning of the God of Abraham, Isaac and Jacob was wasted, for he was separating himself from God's people.

Was it only a few days ago that he had known a place of honor in Egypt? Was it only a few days since he had decided to be the champion of the Hebrew slaves—and had tried to begin? Was it really Moses, the prince of Egypt, who today was hunted by the Egyptians, rejected by the Hebrews—and running from both?

He slowed his pace almost to a halt. He shook his head, swallowed hard and let his broad shoulders slump. Then, more from habit than from new resolve, he resumed his normal pace, straightened his shoulders and held his head high again. He walked as rapidly as he could without attracting attention. He avoided people, kept off main thoroughfares and angled toward the nearest garrisoned outpost. From there it wasn't far to the edge of the wilderness that isolated Egypt from much of the world.

The hostile desert wilderness was an unlikely haven. One man alone scarcely ever lived to cross it, but that mattered little to the prince.

The outpost loomed ahead in the early evening greyness. He gave it a wide berth, walking more rapidly, trying not to think of anything except the urgency of escaping notice— of getting beyond Egypt's border.

Darkness had settled over the world around him; the new

moon had set. He came to a flat-topped acacia tree and leaned against it, feeling he could not take one more step. He stared up at the tree's weathered branches and ran his hand along its trunk. Growing in parched soil, uncared-for by anyone—it was a survivor. The exile nodded in admiration of its stamina. Then he sat down under its protection.

He opened his pack and took out a late supper of dry bread; he drank some water. The sky was lit by stars "as numerous as the sand of the sea." They were taunting symbols of a people that was being oppressed in a calculated plan of annihilation. Those people seemed remote to him now—like the stars—and like the God who made them.

"Elohim . . . El Elyon . . . I'm alone, afraid. My life is wasted." Strange words for a prince.

After a time he unrolled a thin mat and spread it on the sparse grass under the old tree that stood like a lonely sentinel over its tiny oasis. Moses escaped into dreamless sleep. But first he did remember—so many things.

Part Two

The Servant

—————————————————————*16*

> Now Moses was tending the flocks of Jethro his father-in-law,
> the priest of Midian.   *Exodus 3:1*

Moses awoke to bright sunlight, although he had wanted to be on his way by dawn to take advantage of the hours before the desert heat became too oppressive. As he ate fruit and bread from his sack of provisions and drank from his waterskin, he decided on the immediate course he would take.

It clearly seemed best to follow, at a safe distance, the caravan route that wound around the Sinai Peninsula to the coast of the Gulf of Aqabah. That trade route led to Mesopotamia, but he planned to go only as far as Midian, where descendants of Abraham and his second wife, Keturah, lived. Because he shared a common heritage with them, Moses felt he would be welcomed, but he cringed at the thought of a prince reduced to seeking refuge with his semi-nomadic kinsmen.

He knew little about Midian. Egypt wasn't interested in acquiring it as a vassal state because it was remote and unimpressive. Its modest trade was in wool, some copper and turquoise. Moses had sent a few messages concerning those items to Midian during his term as diplomatic scribe, and he remembered how reluctantly his messengers had left on those assignments. It was a hazardous, uncomfortable journey, whether by boat down the western branch of the Red Sea and then overland to the Gulf of Aqabah, or overland the whole way, as he was going. Either choice offered great potential for two extremes, boredom and danger, and no one would have considered sending a messenger on foot alone.

He knew he would encounter scorching days, cold nights and whirling winds driving earthbound clouds of suffocating sand—but at least there would be no Egyptian patrols.

And so he began the lonely trek that would take him around the base of craggy mountains rising sharply from the desert floor, past thorny scrub bushes and acacias growing along dry wadi banks. He would walk over dust and sand and stones and sparse grass—occasionally coming to an oasis where he could rest under palm trees, replenish his water supply and sometimes find dates or pomegranates. He was thankful he was not making the crossing in the season of cloudbursts that added still another fearsome touch to the desert traveler's dangers.

At times he walked on the caravan highway itself, always alert. The sight of approaching traffic would send him scurrying back to the obscurity of the brown, barren, deep-gullied land. During the midday heat he stayed in the shadows of overhanging rocks or retreated into caves in the limestone hills.

With each step the culture of Egypt fell further behind him, but thoughts of his former home nagged at him day and night. Just when he had come into national prominence, he had deliberately brought disgrace on himself. At the beginning of what without doubt would have been a uniquely successful life of power, wealth, ease and pleasure, he chose to identify with slaves—particularly with a runaway slave! Why? What good did it do? He had not helped even one Hebrew! That slave whose life he had spared near Akhetaton would have been captured quickly—arrested and executed for the murder of his hapless Egyptian guard. And what would become of his own family if they were forced from the shelter of Rekhmire's estate?

He would have exchanged the glitter and power of Egypt for the opportunity to be the Lord God's person to lead His people back to Canaan—as his mother had hoped and prayed he would do. But now he had traded his place in Egypt for that of a footsore exile, who sweltered in the oppressive white heat of desert days and shivered in the inhospitable chill of dark desert nights. He had neither Egypt nor Canaan.

He assessed his situation as intolerable, unbearable! His fury was more devastating than his physical deprivations. At times he found caves where he could rest from the searing heat and the wearisome walking, but his thoughts were relentless, ravaging his mind like spike-toothed harrows.

He began to want to pray. He remembered his mother praying—long sessions of praising the Lord God and of petitioning Him. She had tried to teach him to pray. But ever since he was 12 years old the prayers he had heard were complicated chants intoned by Egyptian priests. Supplications made at the temple at On were offered as charms against evil; they had to do with spells and counterspells, and they required magic herbs and potions to make them effective. Moses would not offer such vain worship to Elohim! Unable to think of appropriate words with which to address his God, he offered silence. Wordlessly, earnestly, with childlike hope, he sought guidance and a confirmation of Elohim's presence.

No revelation came; there was no reassuring voice, no soul-satisfying vision. But there did well up inside him a strength that enabled him to endure the present situation, a consuming desire to see beyond it, and a certainty that there was yet something to strive for—to become. Strength, desire and certainty mingled and struggled with discouragement, despair and exhaustion. And he experienced an energizing comfort—a kind of sweet joy—in just meditating on the one God who was so real to his mother. Perhaps this God understood wordless prayers, desolate longing and the desperate need of a new beginning.

One night, abruptly aroused from sleep, he thought he heard the Voice. He listened, holding his breath and unconsciously leaning forward as if that might help capture the elusive sound. Then he laughed quietly at his own eagerness. If El Shaddai ever spoke to him, it would not be in a whisper! He would not have to strain to hear.

He settled back into the quiet darkness, thinking of the marvelous names of God his mother had taught him:

Elohim — God
Yahweh — Life
El Shaddai — Almighty God
Yahweh-yireh — Provider
Adonai — The Lord
El Elyon — Most High God

Moses wondered how many more names there were for his sovereign God. He longed to know them all, for each one emphasized a facet of His being. Knowing His wonderful names meant knowing more about God Himself. Thinking of God became rest and peace for him. Problems and mistakes were temporarily forgotten as his mind and spirit soared while he praised his God for who He is.

The space between Egypt and Midian often seemed unrelated to either past or future. It was a special time—just "now" moments. And Moses learned to share many of those precious moments with the Lord God. He sensed that this intense longing to know more about Him was the real beginning of fellowship with Him! It was a blessed fellowship—encouraging, soothing, comforting, invigorating—bringing always an increased desire for even deeper communion.

Wilderness looks much the same from one day to the next, but it's called by different names in different areas: Shur, Ethan, Sin. Finally, in Paran the majestic Sinai chain dominates the landscape and rises to craggy peaks over 7,000 feet high.

In Paran dust-laden winds howled at him almost daily, but as he neared the place to turn north along the gulf, they quieted. Free from their harassment and now in sight of the brilliant blue of Aqabah's refreshing water, Moses began the last part of his retreat from Mizraim.

His immediate destination was Madian, a small city about 70 miles up the east side of the gulf. If he found no suitable refuge there, he would go on to Ezion-geber, the city to which he had sent messengers in what now seemed like another lifetime. There would be someone in Madian or Ezion-geber who would welcome a multilingual, well-educated, experienced scribe; Moses turned his thoughts toward finding a position that would be in some measure appropriate to his excellent background.

Some miles south of Madian he stopped at a small village. He wanted to rest. He must not arrive at his destination looking and feeling like a haggard, sand-coated pilgrim. He found that the villagers understood the Akkadian language, so communication with them was easy. He slept at the local inn—more comfortably and soundly than he had since the night before he had arrived at Akhetaton.

The next day he purchased new sandals. He bought fruit and cheese. He enjoyed the taste of cool water from ancient springs. He delighted to splash water from tall jugs into large basins for bathing.

Having been alone for so long, he found it a joy to see people go about their daily work—gardeners, potters, weavers, shopkeepers, women who tended babies and who laughed and gossiped as they washed clothes in the Aqabah. He watched children play, laughing and screaming in excitement. One of their favorite games involved two small boys riding on the shoulders of two older boys who ran across an open field with the excited riders tossing a ball back and forth between them. Moses felt a stab of envy; he and Aaron had never been carefree like those boys.

He was grateful for this time of relaxing and healing. He became accustomed to the townspeople and their routines of working, playing and meeting around the well to talk. He knew he was the subject of their conversation many times, but he was careful not to let them know where he came from or why he traveled alone. He let all who wanted to do it provide their own ideas of the "wheres" and "whys."

When he was rested, he left the town, still a stranger there. Madian was only a few days away.

The town well was the traditional place where friends met and strangers were welcomed. Moses went first to the well when he came to Madian.

In a turn of events he never could have anticipated but that reminded him of the story his mother had told him of how Jacob and Rachel met, he defended from ruffian shepherds a beautiful shepherdess and her sisters, who had brought their sheep to the well. The young lady was Zipporah, daughter of the priest of Midian, who presided in its holy city, Madian.

Because of his gallantry Moses was invited into the priest's home. He was impressed by his host, a generous man of dignity and simplicity. His name was Jethro, which, he explained with a childlike bashful pride, means "excellence." Moses thought it was a good name for him. Jethro's hospitality was gracious, and he urged his guest to stay on. He provided comfortable quarters and ample meals and seemed to consider it a real delight to serve as host. He spent considerable time with Moses. He showed him the altar dedicated to the God of Abraham, took him out to see his flocks and introduced him to the townspeople.

And Moses, longing to hear all he could of the Lord God, encouraged Jethro to tell about his priestly duties. The Midianites had developed a system of sacrifice and intercessory prayer to the God of Abraham, and Jethro performed the priestly duties. He spoke of his work in the same way in which he carried it out—with reverence. He knew the traditions of his fathers but had never read the sacred writings that had been taken into Egypt with Jacob. He had never had a vision from the Lord God or heard His voice. Moses had learned more from Jochebed than he could learn from Jethro, yet there was pleasure in discussing with this man what each knew about the God they both worshiped.

After some days Jethro could contain his curiosity no longer. He hadn't asked his guest any questions, and no information had been volunteered.

"You've come from Egypt, judging from your speech, your fine manners and your clothing."

"Yes." Moses owed his host minimal answers but wouldn't supply details unless they were requested.

The request came immediately. "You are going to Damascus?"

"No."

"Babylon?"

"No."

Jethro was becoming embarrassed by his own persistent questioning, but curiosity kept him prodding. "Perhaps Ezion-geber?"

"Not necessarily, although that's a possibility. I'm looking for a place to settle. I'm a skilled scribe, and I speak three languages. I would be willing to stay in Madian if there is need for a scribe. I also can teach mathematics and . . ."

Jethro raised his hand for quiet. "I need another shepherd."

"A shepherd?" Moses spoke the word as Meoris would have, implying that shepherding was an abominable form of slavery.

"A shepherd. Yes, a shepherd." Jethro's face beamed with delight; he was offering Moses a choice occupation!

"I . . . know . . . *nothing* . . . about sheep."

"I will teach you." Jethro's smile widened at the idea of teaching such an impressive man anything.

"A . . . shepherd." Moses repeated the word as if it were a death sentence.

Jethro waited for an answer. Moses tried to sort out his tumultuous thoughts so he could give his host as kind an answer as possible and still say no. With his education and training he would be wasted in such work. He couldn't consider it, even temporarily. It would only delay his getting on with whatever he would be doing the rest of his life. He couldn't waste any more time. The Egyptian prince stiffened; he would go yet that day to Ezion-geber or, as Jethro had suggested earlier, make plans to go on to Damascus or Babylon—where a scribe would be appreciated.

Jethro had given his guest time to think it over, and now he gave him a little encouragement. His voice was low; he chose his words with care. "Abraham was a shepherd. Isaac was a shepherd. And so was Jacob."

Somehow that simple statement about his forefathers surprised Moses. Of course he had known they were herdsmen, but whenever he had pictured them in his mind, he saw them as priests whose sole employment was praying, conversing directly with the Lord God.

The prince's attitude softened noticeably, but his slight smile was not from joy. Moses thought it ironic. At least he could have shepherding in common with the patriarchs.

Jethro called him back from his private thoughts. "I need a shepherd."

"I . . . will serve you . . . well."

Jethro embraced his new shepherd, and Moses felt the embrace of a father.

Early the next morning, as he prepared to go out for his first lesson, he thought of the reactions two women would have to his new occupation. Princess Meoris would be livid! Jochebed would nod her head in delight at this break with the artificial culture of Mizraim; she would see a pattern beginning. God's choice leaders were often taught and tested while in the discipline of tending sheep.

Moses went out to meet Jethro, his new mentor. Jethro made a ceremony of presenting Moses with a shepherd's staff. Moses accepted the tool of his new profession, seeing it as a pitiful reminder of the jeweled scepter he might have received from Egypt. His hand tightened around a crude wooden rod.

—*17*

He led the flock to the far side of the desert and came to Horeb
[Sinai], the mountain of God.   *Exodus 3:1*

Months flowed into years until nearly 40 years had
gone by. Right from the first, Moses had brought his innate
resourcefulness, energy and thoroughness to his work.
Jethro loved him as a son, gave him Zipporah for his wife
and gradually increased his responsibilities with the flocks
until he became the chief shepherd.

Moses was wealthy, the father of two sons and generally
contented. Zipporah took pride in being a good homemaker
and a loving mother. Their marriage was based on respect
for each other; they were comfortable in each other's presence.

The only shadows over their relationship were Moses'
unusual longing for fellowship with his silent God and his
grieving for his enslaved people. Zipporah tried to persuade
her husband to be practical and reasonable. "You've tried
to help your people, but you couldn't. So let someone else
do it. Some of the slaves might even start a rebellion."

"They already have . . . many times . . . and were crushed
even more severely as a result. I feel that somehow I . . ."

"My father says our spiritual requirements are to trust
God and to obey Him. And we are to pray to Him and praise
Him, of course. But . . . why should you be caught up in
dreams about hearing God speak? I think that might even
be presumptuous!"

Zipporah thought her philosophy was sound, and she
voiced it frequently. She had more patience in repeating it

than her husband had in hearing it repeated so many times.

Presumptuous or not, Moses clung to his deep, deep desire to hear God's voice. It became for him a consuming need.

At times he remembered the gods and goddesses of Egypt—their grotesque appearance, their depravity, their impotence. He wondered how the intelligent, sophisticated Egyptians could have given any of them serious thought, much less worship! And who had decided what they should look like?

No one would dare make an image of his God. No one could cast in metal or carve from stone the essence of His being.

One of his most bitter regrets was that he had not been able to locate and read the records the patriarchs had written, at the Lord God's direction, concerning His dealings with them. Another regret was that he had none of the elders with him to tell more of what they had learned from their own forefathers about El Shaddai.

Occasionally Moses accompanied Jethro when he went to make ritual sacrifices for his people and when he went to the altar for long intercessions on their behalf. Moses felt a semblance of worship at these times, but he knew that fellowship with God had been much more personal for his ancestors, and he wanted no less for himself.

He was no longer afraid of Egyptian spies. Both the Egyptians and the Hebrews must have long since considered him dead; few would even remember him after such a span of time. He often met caravans that stopped at Madian on their way to Mesopotamia or to Egypt to leave off supplies of food, grain, cloth and trinkets and to pick up wool, copper and turquoise. He wasn't interested in the merchandise, but he liked to hear news from beyond the sanctuary town of Madian—from beyond the borders of the land of Midian.

A large caravan had come in from Egypt, and Moses arranged to go into town to talk with the caravaneer.

"Do you bring news of any importance?"

"Yes, big news from Egypt."

"A new temple or a new pyramid?"

"No, a new Pharaoh. Rameses is dead."

"Rameses . . . dead?"

"That's what I said. And there's more news." The informant grew quiet, enjoying the suspense he had created.

Moses looked unconcerned, not wanting to appear too interested.

The caravaneer broke the silence; his eagerness to tell his story overcame his attempted reserve. "There are uprisings in Nubia, Libya and Canaan. They all want to shake off Egyptian influence now, before the new Pharaoh gets firm control. And besides all the rebels in outlying places, he has strong opposition right in his own palace and . . ."

"Who is the new Pharaoh?"

"Merneptah."

Merneptah! Moses remembered him as well as if he had seen him only the day before. Meoris had considered this son of Pharaoh's favorite great wife the only serious rival for the throne she coveted for Moses. Merneptah was arrogant and as ruthless as his father. Moses hoped the opposition would be successful in overthrowing his reign before it could get entrenched.

"I said *Merneptah!*" The caravaneer thought his information was not receiving proper attention.

"Yes, I heard you. You told me the new Pharaoh's name, but you didn't say who his opposition was."

"Oh . . . a noisy few. I hear it's some scribes and a priest or two—and old Rameses' daughter and a prince named Kha."

"Do they have a chance?"

"Only if they do it quickly. If Merneptah has time to reinforce his position with, say . . . bribery . . . or intimidation, . . . then the others had better run for their lives. I hear he can be more cruel than Rameses."

"How do the Hebrew slaves fare?"

The caravaneer, already intrigued at the interest of this shepherd in Egypt's politics, was further surprised at this last question. And Moses, who habitually guarded his identity from strangers, was surprised at his own questions.

The answer came slowly as the man scrutinized this inquisitive Midianite carefully. "Merneptah continues the building programs of Egypt. There are plenty of Hebrews in chains to get the work done."

Moses lost his desire for further conversation. "Your news has been interesting, my friend. Peace to you, and a successful journey."

He hurried back to Jethro and asked for his priestly prayers for their kinsmen.

It had taken years for him to come to any kind of terms with his failure regarding his people, but gradually he had even come to feel a certain relief at being free from the challenge of helping them. Now old tensions resurfaced and engulfed him with gnawing feelings of responsibility and frustration. Zipporah's renewed arguments that he disassociate himself from the Hebrews' problems were ignored.

Jethro noticed that his son-in-law had become more withdrawn, serious, preoccupied, his mind filled with emotions he did not share with anyone else. He could not solve Moses' problems, but he offered practical help—hard work.

"I've been thinking it would be a good thing to divide our flocks, Moses. I'll oversee the ones that remain here until I can find another shepherd to take charge of them. I want you to establish another grazing center in the southern peninsula. It will mean more than a hundred miles between my tents and yours, but that's the nearest suitable grazing area beyond this one. I would trust few men to take the flocks that far."

Moses sensed that Jethro was trying to motivate him to fight his despondency with action. Placing his hands on the older man's shoulders, he found it possible to smile. "There's a saying I learned years ago: 'As you say, I will do.' "

During the next weeks the flocks were divided. Supplies were purchased and loaded on a pack train. Undershepherds were assigned to go with Moses to the region of the Sinai mountains.

Moses thought the land toward Ezion-geber would have been better. Almost any land would be better than that sun-scorched earth in Paran's wilderness. But with the old sorrow on his mind again, he didn't bother to engage Jethro in conversation about the matter.

Zipporah thought it would be better for her to stay with their sons, Gershom and Eliezer, at the home camp of Jethro until the new headquarters was established. Moses agreed and promised to come back for them soon.

It was a good time for the move. It was spring, and there had been a heavy deluge of rain. Wadis were flowing full; pasture grass and wild flowers flourished near these vital veins of water. Moses directed his men to dig wells into the rock beneath the shallow soil so that when the wadis dried up again, they still would have water available.

He constantly scouted for the best nearby grazing areas, supervised the sheep and the shepherds with wisdom and concern and found satisfaction in being the head of the pastoral community at Sinai.

Spring gave way to early summer. It was hot and dry, and the pasture was failing. He discussed the problems with his chief aide, Qehat.

"Jethro's flocks will not do well here. I've never seen such meager pasture or such thin, rocky soil in all the years I've herded sheep."

"There's better pasture up there, but no one will go." Qehat nodded casually toward a mountain on the horizon.

"Pasture? Where? On that tallest mountain?"

"Yes."

"If there's good pasture, why won't the shepherds use it?"

"Because . . . they're afraid." Qehat looked at Moses as though his question had an obvious answer. Then he turned to squint intensely at that special mountain.

Moses, amused at the superstitious shepherd, probed for more information. "Why are they afraid?"

"Deity lives there!"

"Which deity?"

"The great God, Elohim."

"Has anyone ever seen Him?"

"No."

"Has this God spoken to anyone? Has He told people not to trespass on the slopes of His mountain?"

"Some say so."

"Who?"

"Tradition says so. We don't question tradition."

"Why not?"

"Because we're afraid."

The questioning had come full circle; the discussion had reached an inconclusive ending.

Moses thought for a time about the high pastures on the side of the grandest mountain in the Sinai chain; he thought of the superstition—and he was intrigued. He began to understand why Jethro had sent him to this place. His father-in-law hadn't underestimated his desire to be confronted by the Lord God!

The next week he told Qehat he was going on ahead to check out the grazing possibilities on that mountain.

"Not up on that sacred mountain!"

"Yes."

"Alone?"

"Do you want to go with me?"

"No!"

"Then I'll go alone."

18

Then he said, "I am the God of your father, the God of Abraham, the God of Isaac and the God of Jacob."   *Exodus 3:6*

Moses was tired when he reached the base of that highest mountain. It was farther from camp than he had thought; distances are deceptive across ravines and around craggy mounds. It was nearly dark, so he wouldn't climb at all until morning, but he studied the sacred mountain as well as he could in the brief twilight. It looked sparsely green with grass that could provide little pasture on its steep sides. Scraggly bushes and a lone tree here and there pushed through crevices between cliffs. It didn't look as though it would be worth the effort to check it out further. But if he didn't, Qehat would think he had been afraid.

He threw his bed mat onto the ground and lay down, wondering why he cared what an undershepherd thought about his courage—or lack of it. The sky was a dark-domed setting for stars. Moses thought there must be a slave in Egypt for each of those sparkling lights, long ago designated by the Lord God as symbols for the multiplied seed of Abraham. His eyes were wet with tears before he slept.

Sunrise flooded the dreary brown plain with a rose-rich light, and the massive mountains seemed to tower halfway to the sky. As Moses ate breakfast, he studied the particular mountain he would challenge. After he had eaten, he sat still for some time, just staring at it. He began to question again the wisdom—the sanity—of trying to scale it. Even if there were patches of good pasture, great herds of sheep couldn't be led up those craggy precipices.

He could not justify the energy and time his climb would take, but as he made ready to begin the ascent, he trembled with undeniable excitement. Pasture was incidental. He would climb Sinai because the Midianites might be right!

It seemed probable that if God were to make His home on earth, it would be on such a mountain. This rugged, gigantic mass of stone defied description. Let the Egyptian Pharaohs revel in their 40- and 60-foot statues, in costly temples and pyramids. Moses found it interesting to picture them all lined up like toys in front of the spectacular grandeur of Sinai. The God who created all things must laugh at the pompous strutting of men who aspire to greatness by piling up blocks!

He had to climb before the day became warmer; it would be difficult enough without the assaulting heat that would come in a few hours. As he bent his shoulders forward on an especially steep grade he thought how the Lord God must laugh not only at the builders of pyramids, statues and temples but also at a man with nothing better to do than climb a nearly inaccessible mountain.

After two grueling hours he stopped to consider some questions: Was he being duped by Midianite superstition? Did he really fear being thought afraid to climb? Had he seen any pasture worth coming here for? Why waste any more energy or time—why not turn back? The questions darted at him like sweat bees. He didn't have logical answers for his questions, but he would go on a little further.

The way grew steeper. He turned to look over the path on which he had come and shuddered to think he had to go back that same way. Going down would be even worse! He could imagine Qehat and the other shepherds talking:

"Why does the old man want to climb that mountain anyway?"

"Does he want to worship God or defy Him?"

"Maybe he just wants to find out if He's there."

"Probably he only wants to prove he's still brave and surefooted."

"Well, if he isn't surefooted, we've seen the last of him."

Moses sat down to rest and to enjoy the spectacular view. The enormous cliffs around him were serrated from ages of assault by dust-laden winds and veined by torrential rains. The plain below looked endless, the sky above, infinite.

Scarcely a third of the way up, he felt more a part of the mountains and sky than of the world of men and their miseries and prosaic affairs. The very air was different at this height, and he breathed deeply of it.

He looked down at the lavish expanse of wilderness below, then at the awesome mountains around him. He wanted to memorize it so he could see the grandeur, feel the majesty of it all again when he was back down below, plodding from pasture to pasture with sheep, sheep, sheep.

Midday heat prevented his going farther, so he sought out a protective ledge and sat in its shade to wait for the cooler time in late afternoon. It was good to sit down. He rested his eyes but soon opened them again to study his surroundings—the solid, immovable, impersonal, towering rocks and cliffs.

He was not prepared for what suddenly filled his vision. Dazed and disbelieving, he was drawn toward the wondrous sight!

The angel of the Lord appeared to him in flames from within a bush. Moses saw that though the bush was on fire, it did not burn up.

When the Lord saw that he had gone over to look, God called to him from within the bush, "Moses, Moses!"

And Moses said, "Here I am."

"Do not come any closer," God said. "Take off your sandals, for the place where you are standing is holy ground." Then He said, "I am the God of your father, the God of Abraham, the God of Isaac, and the God of Jacob." At this, Moses hid his face, because he was afraid to look at God.

The atmosphere was pervaded with exquisite peace, energized with delight and anticipation. The words of the Lord God had the ring of music, thunder and rushing waters; His voice was like no other sound with which Moses could even begin to compare it. It was the voice of the one God—the God of Abraham, Isaac and Jacob—and by His own statement, the God of "your father." That meant Amram! Moses would reflect later on that startling revelation. He could imagine the Lord God claiming as His special people the giants of faith, the venerated patriarchs; but in that same sentence He had said "your father." Scarcely anyone even knew Amram, but in God's sight he was just as much a person of concern as Abraham, Isaac and Jacob were! Oh, blessed God of Israel! Then it followed—He even was the God of Moses!

The Lord God continued to speak to him, telling of His compassion for His people in chains, telling him that their time of suffering was at an end and they were to go back to their "good and spacious land."

Moses listened breathlessly, his heart pounding with joy. Then the Lord God's next words evoked a very different emotion as Moses heard, "I am sending *you* to Pharaoh to bring my people the Israelites out of Egypt."

There was no mistaking those words. Moses' mind reeled with two questions: Are you sure you mean me? How can it be done? In a voice made all but inaudible by reverent fear, he asked, "Who am I, that I should go to Pharaoh and bring the Israelites out of Egypt?"

And God said, "I will be with you. And this will be the sign to you that it is I who have sent you: When you have brought the people out of Egypt, you will worship God on this mountain."

Moses said to God, "Suppose I go to the Israelites and say to them, 'The God of your fathers has sent me to you,' and they ask me, 'What is his name?' Then what shall I tell them?"

God said to Moses, "I am who I am. This is what you are to say to the Israelites: 'I AM has sent me to you.' "

The resonant utterance of that name was so powerful that Moses felt drained of his own strength and filled with fresh new enabling power. He pondered the name—so simple a child could say it, so profound that no philosopher could exhaust its meaning. The names of God had long been precious to Moses, each one giving its own revelation of Him, but now there was one name above them all, and he had heard it spoken by the only One who could claim it.

And that One went on talking to Moses for a long while. He commanded Moses to return to Egypt to tell the Israelites that the time of their redemption had come. He promised miracles and wonders that would convince the Egyptians to let His people go. He said the Israelites would leave the land of their captivity boldly—with gold and silver and clothing!

Moses listened intently. He never would forget one single word or the cadence of the Voice he had waited so long to hear. But the message was so startling that it was difficult to comprehend, and Moses dared to ask for more assurance.

"What if they do not believe me or listen to me and say, 'The Lord did not appear to you'?"

Then the Lord said to him, "What is that in your hand?"

"A staff," he replied.

The Lord said, "Throw it on the ground."

Moses threw it on the ground and it became a snake, and he ran from it. Then the Lord said to him, "Reach out your hand and take it by the tail."

So Moses reached out and took hold of the snake, and it turned back into a staff in his hand. "This," said the Lord, "is so that they may believe that the Lord, the God of their fathers—the God of Abraham, the God of Isaac and the God of Jacob—has appeared to you."

Then the Lord said, "Put your hand inside your cloak." So Moses put his hand into his cloak, and when he took it out, it was leprous, like snow.

"Now put it back into your cloak," he said. So Moses put his hand back into his cloak, and when he took it out, it was restored, like the rest of his flesh.

Then the Lord said, "If they do not believe you or pay attention to the first miraculous sign, they may believe the second. But if they do not believe these two signs or listen to you, take some water from the Nile and pour it on the dry ground. The water you take from the river will become blood on the ground."

Moses said to the Lord, "O Lord, I have never been eloquent, neither in the past nor since you have spoken to your servant. I am slow of speech and tongue."

The Lord said to him, "Who gave man his mouth? . . . Now go; I will help you speak and will teach you what to say."

But Moses said, "O Lord, please send someone else to do it."

Then the Lord's anger burned against Moses and He said, "What about your brother, Aaron the Levite? I know he can speak well. He is already on his way to meet you, and his heart will be glad when he sees you. You shall speak to him and put words in his mouth; I will help both of you speak and will teach you what to do. He will speak to the people for you, but it will be as if he were your mouth and as if you were God to him. But take this staff in your hand so you can perform miraculous signs with it."

Then the Voice was still. Moses remained motionless for a long time, letting the unimaginable thing that had just happened become impressed on his mind. He reviewed it all, step by step.

The Lord God had spoken to him. He had heard divine promises, seen miraculous signs. He had been given an assignment—and had refused it! He had been offered the assignment again, with Aaron as his helper. And finally, he had accepted his calling by silent consent.

And so, as his father and mother had predicted and as he had hoped and dreamed, he was in fact to be the Lord God's instrument to lead His people home. It seemed he had always known it, yet now that it had been made clear, he was having difficulty believing it.

Once as a young child, Moses had expressed disbelief that the sacred writings of the patriarchs could be inspired by the invisible God. Jochebed had explained that there is a vast difference between willful, defiant unbelief and the inability to *understand* the things of the Lord God. Now Moses applied that lesson to this inexplicable, marvelous moment. He prayed that the Lord God would enable him to believe what he might never understand!

Then his thoughts became jumbled, out of sequence. He would lead the Israelites out of Egypt to Mt. Sinai to worship the Lord God. . . . He looked at his staff and was relieved to see that it was the familiar one he had used for many years. . . . Aaron was on his way to meet him. . . . The Israelites would not only be allowed to leave Egypt, but they would leave with plunder of gold, silver and fine clothing. . . . He examined his hand to make certain there was no sign of leprosy. . . . The water of the Nile would turn to blood! . . . His people . . . their God-promised land of milk and honey!

He stood up, closed his eyes and put his hands over his ears to shut out any further sight or sound for some moments. Then he raised his hands to the heavens and praised his God.

He knelt again at the bush that had been wrapped in glory. He touched its leaves; they were green and fresh.

He stayed on his knees for a long time, looking at the sky, concentrating on the words he had just heard—and on the blessed One who had spoken them.

His mind returned to its customary precise reckoning, and he thought through in orderly fashion the life-changing experience just past. Then as he prepared to return to his flocks, his mind was quieted, and from all the challenging information he had been given one phrase became his strength and song, the source of his comfort and of his daring: The Lord God had said, "I will be with you."

"With you . . . with *you!*" These were words to remember—a promise to live by!

19

> The Egyptians will know that I am the Lord when I stretch out
> my hand against Egypt and bring the Israelites out of it.
>
> *Exodus 7:5*

God had always been with him. Looking back over his life, Moses reviewed the evidence:

The Hebrew child, miraculously saved from infanticide, became one of the most learned men of his time, successful in diplomacy and in battle and heir-apparent to the Egyptian throne. It had taken 40 years.

The shepherd in Midian, having forsaken the riches of Egypt, discovered that greatness—or worthlessness—has to do with one's relationship with the Lord God. It took 40 more years.

Then for his last 40 years, he consistently had claimed the divinely promised "with you" as he worked out his calling. Both his magnificent accomplishments and his patient plodding with those of little faith through needless wilderness wanderings were the result of taking God at His Word!

Now at the age of 120, he was indulging in the privilege of those who have lived a long life—thinking back over his years.

As soon as he and Aaron got back to Egypt, they went to the city of Rameses and called the elders of the Hebrews together. Moses found that he already was regarded by many of the people as a legend; they found it hard to believe he could be alive and in their midst—and with a message from the Lord God that was meant for each one of them.

Their deliverance was at hand. Aaron faithfully reported all that God had told Moses from the burning bush on the sacred mountain.

Moses, nodding affirmation of what Aaron said, waited until his brother finished speaking. Then with a reverence that communicated both a profound faith and a holy joy, he confirmed Aaron's words with the God-ordained signs. He threw his shepherd's staff on the ground, and it became a serpent. After the elders had gasped in astonishment and fear, Moses grabbed it by the tail, and it became the staff again. He put the hand that had held the staff inside his cloak, drew it out and let the men see it was leprous. Then he put it inside the cloak again and brought it out for everyone to see—whole and cleansed.

The men who watched these miracles showed different degrees of awe. Some were openmouthed; a few were on their knees; the eyes of many were brimming with tears; a small group of older men had raised their arms in praise to El Shaddai.

There was one more startling sign to demonstrate that Moses was God's appointed servant. Aaron handed his brother a vial of water, drawn earlier from the Nile. Moses poured it out, and as it splashed onto the ground, it became blood.

Spontaneous praying and praising of the Lord God broke out, and all through the night there was a sharing of joy and hope. Egyptian sentries heard the shouting and singing, the weeping and laughing—and they were mystified.

The elders quickly passed the news to the rest of the people, and rejoicing swept through all the slave settlements in Mizraim. The sentries also passed along the news of the unparalleled celebration, and Egypt was alerted that the long-rumored slave rebellion might be starting.

When Moses confronted his old rival, Merneptah, with the Lord God's command, the new Pharaoh arrogantly rejected it. Moses had expected a rebuff and was prepared to deal with it. But Merneptah's cruel reprisal for Moses' demand came swiftly with no warning and no escape. Brickyard workers, now the major part of the slave labor force, were to make the same number of bricks as before, but without straw being provided for them. Since it was impossible to glean straw and make bricks at the same time, quotas were not met, and Israelite foremen were brutally lashed while their helpless work crews were forced to look on.

Glad hope in the hearts of the people was erased by anguish and anger and the gnawing question, Why?

Even Moses became discouraged. He saw personal defeat in this first phase of his duel with Merneptah, and he chafed under the criticism of his kinsmen. Before when he tried to help and failed, he had run away. This time he would not. He called on his Lord, who was "with him."

"O Lord, why have you brought trouble on this people? Is this why you sent me? Ever since I went to Pharaoh to speak in your name, he has brought trouble upon this people, and you have not rescued your people at all."

The Lord God answered His servant, "Now you will see what I will do to Pharaoh: Because of My mighty hand he will let them go; because of My mighty hand he will drive them out of his country."

Then God gave Moses a message for his people:

> I am the Lord and I will bring you out from under the yoke of the Egyptians. I will free you from being slaves to them and will redeem you with an outstretched arm with mighty acts of judgment. I will take you as my own people, and I will be your God. Then you will know that I am the Lord your God, who brought you out from under the yoke of the Egyptians. And I will bring you to the land I swore with uplifted hand to give to Abraham, to Isaac and to Jacob. I will give it to you as a possession. I am the Lord.

No one who heard the Voice speak those words would be fearful of a tyrannical Pharaoh or discouraged for long by grumbling kinsmen.

But even a radiant, confident Moses found that Merneptah continued to disdain messages from a god he refused to recognize, and the Israelites still cowered in their agony that was more real to them than promises—even the Lord God's promises.

As for Moses, he was convinced that neither the scorn of Egyptian royalty nor the discouragement of slaves would keep the Lord God from accomplishing what He was ready to do.

In 10 God-ordained assaults, interspersed with warnings and opportunities for Pharaoh to relent, the gods and goddesses of Mizraim were brought down.

The first attack negated the Nile, which was itself a chief god, and proved the impotence of Khnum, guardian of the river source, and Osiris, the god whose blood stream that mighty river was said to be.

In successive waves others were vanquished: the frog deity, Hapi; the earth god, Geb, whose dust became gnats; Uatchit, the fly god. An epidemic of murrain attacked animals and defeated Mneuvus, the cow god; Hathor with the cow's head; Apis, the bull; and others.

The Egyptians were terrified. Then they became personally and painfully involved as a plague of boils infested them. They called in vain to Imhotep and Serapis for healing. Their sky god, Nut, and their god of the atmosphere, Shu, were powerless against the deluge of hail and fire sent by the great God of Israel. Serpia could not protect them against locusts and so forfeited the role of protector against those voracious insects.

Then darkness came, so thick that it could be felt. Re, Amon-Re, and Aten—the sun gods—were discredited; Thoth, the moon god, was conquered.

The gods and goddesses of the Egyptian pantheon were of no effect against the one God who empowered Moses. Even Pharaoh's magicians warned him, "This is the finger of God." But Merneptah's heart was hard, and he would not listen.

There was yet a god who had not been challenged: Pharaoh himself and his firstborn son, who, as heir to the throne, was considered to be one with his father.

A chilling awe filled the hearts of the Israelites who listened in breathless quiet as Moses told them of God's final judgment about to be released on their captors. The Lord would pass through Egypt to strike down every firstborn. But just as God's people in Goshen had been spared the former plagues that had overwhelmed the Egyptians, so they would be safe from this plague of death if they followed the Lord God's specific command.

Moses gave them God's instructions carefully. The people understood beyond doubt what was required of them. On the 10th of that month they were to select a male lamb. It was to be scrutinized carefully until the 14th day, to make certain it was without blemish. It then was to be slaughtered at twilight, and the meat was to be roasted with bitter herbs and entirely eaten. If a family was too small to eat the lamb, they should plan to share the meal with another family. Bread was to be made without yeast. They should eat quickly, with sandals on their feet and a walking staff in hand to indicate readiness to move out.

During the night of the 14th of Nisan, God's final judgment would fall on Mizraim—and Israel would observe the first Passover meal.

The people knelt and worshiped quietly. Reverent fear of the angel of death was apparent; so was childlike faith that when they responded to God's command they would not die.

It was late, but Moses repeated his message of the awesome event before dismissing the people. And in his restatement there were words to encourage them to think of the time when they would finally be beyond the reach of the Egyptians:

> When the Lord goes through the land to strike down the Egyptians, He will see the blood on the top and the sides of the doorframe and will pass over that doorway, and He will not permit the destroyer to enter your houses and strike you down.
>
> Obey these instructions as a lasting ordinance for you and your descendants. When you enter the land that the Lord will give you as He promised, observe this ceremony. And when your children ask you, "What does this ceremony mean to you?"

then tell them, "It is the Passover sacrifice to the Lord, who passed over the houses of the Israelites in Egypt and spared our homes when He struck down the Egyptians."

As God had said, so it was done.

Merneptah sent for Moses. An anguished, tormented man was ready to yield to the command of the God of Moses.

The two men faced each other for the last time. Rivals since they were young men and rivals still, they belonged to two vastly different worlds.

With great effort the Pharaoh, Lord of the Diadem of the Vulture and of the Snake, Exalted Ruler of Egypt, stood erect and raised an imperious arm to point in rage at Moses. "Up! Leave my people, you and the Israelites! Go, worship the Lord as you have requested. Take your flocks and herds, as you have said, and go!"

His arm fell limp at his side; his shoulders sagged as if under enormous burdens. Merneptah's voice was pleading now: "And also bless me."

He stood bereaved, sovereign of a grieving people in a devastated land with a ruined economy, begging for a blessing he had been offered but had rejected time after time.

The Egyptians shared their king's desire for the Israelites to leave their land quickly! To win their favor, and perhaps the favor of their all-powerful God, they gave them lavish gifts of silver, gold and fine clothing to take with them.

The Israelites also took with them the bones of Joseph, to be buried in Canaan in accord with his request made centuries before.

Each person preparing to leave had personal memories of Mizraim to take along. Moses' own thoughts included Princess Meoris. He had wanted to see her during the six months just past, but it had been impossible. She had served the cause of Israel well, and Moses believed that the Lord God would watch over her in loving protection. He thought, too, of graves he had never visited—those of Jochebed and Amram. He remembered the gentle strength of his mother, her teachings and her example of courage and faith. He was comforted by the knowledge of her reunion with Amram shortly after he had gone to Midian; Aaron had told him of it.

When the actual exodus began, the Israelites left as conquerors, but the battle had been the Lord's.

By day the Lord went ahead of them in a pillar of cloud to guide them on their way and by night in a pillar of fire to give them light, so that they could travel by day or night. Neither the pillar of cloud by day nor the pillar of fire by night left its place in front of the people.

They moved to Succoth, then to Etham, then back to Pi Hahiroth—between Migdol and the sea, opposite Baal Zephon. They camped beside the narrow western arm of the Red Sea.

Some of the elders murmured to each other about the unlikely place to which the luminous cloud had led them. The conversation between Shapher and Zior was typical of many.

Shapher slowly squinted at the horizon in all directions. He shook his head, tightened his lips and shook his head again.

"You are anxious about something?" Zior was familiar with his friend's ability to borrow trouble when he had no ready supply of it.

"Aren't you?"

"No."

"You should be. We're in a trap! We've camped in the wrong place this time."

"It couldn't be wrong. We followed the guiding cloud . . . so why should we worry?"

"Zior . . ." Shapher tried to be patient, "God gave us the cloud, but didn't He also give us the gift of common sense?"

Zior grinned, "I suppose so. At least He gave common sense to most of us."

"Then if we determine that this is a dangerous place, we have to ignore either God's gift of the cloud . . . or His gift of common sense." Shapher shrugged, feeling he had won the argument.

"To me, it seems that common sense *is* to follow the cloud . . . since that's God's command. It's foolish to disobey."

Shapher was enraged. "Stand up!"

Zior scrambled to his feet, wondering if he was being challenged to a fight. He tensed in readiness for it.

"What do you see in front of you? Describe it!"

"I see the range of Baal-Zephon's mountains . . . grand and impassable."

"Make a quarter turn. What do you see now? Describe it."

"Migdol's vast wasteland . . . sand."

"And on the third side . . ."

"The Red Sea."

"Zior, think! If we are attacked by marauders, would you suggest that our multitude of people take their possessions and their flocks and run out into the sandy desert . . . or up the cliffs of the mountains . . . or into the sea?"

Zior didn't answer. He looked up toward the cloud again, but his face began to reflect Shapher's concern.

20

> In your unfailing love you will lead the people you have re-
> deemed. In your strength you will guide them to your holy
> dwelling.   *Exodus 15:13*

M oses' scouts rushed into camp with the news.
Six hundred of Pharaoh's best chariots, along with other
chariots and foot soldiers, were bearing down on the un-
armed camp!

The Israelites, hemmed in on two sides and with the sea
at their backs, seemed to be facing certain annihilation. They
confronted Moses.

"Was it because there were no graves in Egypt that you
brought us to the desert to die?"

"What have you done to us?"

"It would have been better for us to serve the Egyptians
than to die in the desert!"

Moses was not intimidated by their fears or their questions. "It's madness to despair of God's providence! In the
worst distress, such as this, we should increase our hope
that God will help us. He has led us to this narrow place
. . . that He might deliver us out of otherwise unsurmount-
able difficulties . . . that He might demonstrate again His
power and His protection over us.

"He will show us that the force of the Egyptian army
against us is as nothing. These mountains can be made level
ground; even the sea can become dry land!"

The people grew more quiet as Moses further challenged
them. "Do not be afraid. Stand firm and you will see the
deliverance the Lord will bring you today. The Egyptians

you see today you will never see again. The Lord will fight for you; you need only to be still."

Moses called out to his Lord and ordered the people to prepare to move.

The Egyptians had come within sight of the Israelites. Their general decided it was too late in the day to begin the massacre; his men were tired. And it was fascinating to contemplate the mental and emotional frenzy of their victims, boxed in with no escape.

The Lord responded to Moses' faith-filled plea: "Raise your staff and stretch out your hand over the sea to divide the water so that the Israelites can go through the sea on dry ground."

The great pillar of cloud moved from in front and stood behind them, coming between the Egyptian army and the Israelites. Throughout the night the cloud brought darkness to one side and light to the other side; so neither went near the other all night long.

The people, urged on by their leaders and by their own terror, moved swiftly, yet it took more than 10 hours for them and their herds and all their possessions to reach the other side of that fork of the Red Sea.

They would always remember the sound of that strong east wind and the sight of the divided water—foaming and swirling—held back while they hurried between the high walls. They would forever recall the sounds of noisy confusion as the cloud lifted and the Egyptians saw that their prey had escaped through the night and the early morning hours.

Unnerved commanders tried to mount a swift pursuit. Foot soldiers put on their armor. Chariots were prepared. When the army was ready to advance, conflicting orders were shouted, causing the charioteers to mill around, wasting precious time. Even the most experienced drivers had difficulty maneuvering in the chaos; they swerved to avoid dangerous entanglements of wheels, sometimes unsuccessfully. The commanders became still more frantic.

When order was restored, the general confidently led his procession into the path made for the people of the one God.

In a single, sudden rush the water slammed back to its place, covering chariots, horsemen, foot soldiers, commanders, and the general. Instantly the wind was calm, and the waves lapped gently, washing bodies of Egyptian soldiers up on the shore.

Excitement swelled through the ranks of the people, thankful to be alive and to be free from long-time oppressors—thankful, so thankful, for the protection of their God, whose Word is infallible, who was with them in omnipotence!

Shouts released their tensions. There was music, singing and dancing—joy such as only a divinely redeemed people can experience!

Moses led the congregation in a jubilant song to the Lord. It was rich with words about the Red Sea victory in particular, but it also was to offer comfort to Israel through all time:

> I will sing to the Lord, for he is highly exalted.
> The horse and its rider he has hurled into the sea.
> The Lord is my strength and my song; he has become my salvation.
> He is my God, and I will praise him, my father's God, and I will exalt him.
> Who among the gods is like you, O Lord?
> Who is like you—majestic in holiness, awesome in glory, working wonders?
> In your unfailing love you will lead the people you have redeemed.
> In your strength you will guide them to your holy dwelling.

The music of a million voices raised a sacrifice of praise to the Lord God. The sound filled the earth around and the skies above.

Into the silence that followed came the gentle ring of a tambourine. As Miriam held the instrument high over her head and tapped out a soft rhythm, she began to sing an echo of the song of Moses:

> Sing to the Lord, for he is highly exalted.
> The horse and its rider He has hurled into the sea.

She sang for the girl who had tossed a straw mat in anger and vowed to escape slavery. She sang for the young woman who held that determination through years of hard work and heartbreak. She sang for the woman—and all her sisters—who now was free!

Soon the camp was filled with the muted bell-like sounds of thousands of tambourines as other women followed Miriam's lead. The chorus was repeated again and again: "Sing to the Lord, for He is highly exalted."

Crisis ended. Celebration ended. The Israelites began the practical task of picking up Egyptian weapons and armor that had washed ashore. They would go on into the wilderness providentially armed.

Moses supervised the work, feeling a surprising empathy for the fallen Egyptian general. If he had stayed in Egypt as general of the army, or if he had become a king who surely would have led his men into battle, he would be lying on the shore of the Red Sea, not feeling its gentle waves, not seeing the sun overhead, oblivious even of defeat. And the Lord God would have chosen another one to lead His people to Canaan!

Moses, servant of God, raised his arms heavenward in allegiance, surrender and praise.

21

> In accordance with your great love, forgive the sin of these people, just as you have pardoned them from the time they left Egypt until now. *Numbers 14:19*

Even though the Egyptians had been defeated, the wilderness years were filled with almost constant warfare. Sometimes there were battles with actual enemies such as the wildly fierce Amalekites, the army from Gilead, or the Amorites. Sometimes the quarrels were among the people themselves. Sometimes the foe was hunger and thirst.

But most often, the struggle was with inner fears, rebellion and self-pity. When troubles came, the people would blame Moses, sometimes becoming so incensed that they threatened to stone him to death. Time after time the recalcitrant people added their own unthinking cruelty to Moses' burden.

He seldom wasted time refuting their accusations; instead, he turned to his God, expecting His help.

When the people murmured about bitter water at Marah in the desert of Shur, the Lord showed Moses a piece of wood. He threw it into the water, and the water became sweet.

When the food supply ran out halfway between Elim and Sinai, the people could have exercised faith or complained to Moses. They did the latter, and he referred it to his Lord. This time the immediate answer was quail, which came flying in vast numbers very low over the land. The people easily netted them, prepared a feast, and ate to excess. The Lord God's long-term answer for their provision was a gift of daily food—a perfectly balanced, heavenly food that tasted like honey and sweet spices. They called it manna (in Hebrew, *mān*, from *mān hū* meaning "What is it?").

Moses paused in his reverie. The last 40 years had been so eventful that just remembering them was strenuous. And he scarcely had begun to call up even the major events. The afternoon was warm, and he thought he might take a short nap. He went to his tent to lie down. Sleep did not come, but in the seclusion of his own quarters he remembered more scenes from the past.

Rephidim . . . Rephidim. He closed his misty eyes as he thought again of that place in a long wadi that led into the high central table land. There had been no rain for months, and they were surrounded by dry desolation—yellowish sand dotted with low bushes and piles of rocks. The people were tired, thirsty and discouraged. Moses heard their angry voices. First they muttered, then moaned, then became violent toward him, charging him with neglect and with not caring about their distress. They picked up stones to kill the man who was just as thirsty as they were!

Moses cried out to his Lord, "What am I to do with these people? They are almost ready to stone me!"

The Lord answered, "Walk on ahead of the people. Take with you some of the elders of Israel and take in your hand the staff with which you struck the Nile, and go. I will stand there before you by the rock at Horeb. Strike the rock, and water will come out of it for the people to drink."

Lying alone in the quiet of his tent, Moses trembled as he relived his awareness of the Lord God's invisible presence by the rock that he struck. The rock opened. Life-giving water gushed from its side. That mysterious, marvelous, riven rock—and the presence of the Lord—made drinking the sweet, clear water a blessed experience.

They had just moved out from Rephidim, refreshed by drinking from the Lord God's fountain, when they were attacked by Amalekites. Those fearsome descendants of Esau swooped down on the descendants of Jacob to destroy them or, at the very least, to block their way into Canaan.

Moses delegated the leadership of the Israelites' amateur army to Joshua. Moses himself, along with Aaron and Hur, went to the top of a nearby hill for the crucial work of watching and praying. He held the staff of God high in victory through the long, battle-weary hours. When the staff became too heavy, his companions held his hands up—until Joshua and his men were able to accomplish the victory that the raised staff proclaimed!

Moses wondered if it were still there—the stone altar he had built at that place and named *Yahweh-nissi* (Yahweh is my Banner).

It was no afternoon for sleeping. Moses got up and walked toward the tabernacle, remembering the place where the Lord God had given him the detailed instructions for building it—Mount Sinai!

As the mountain of God in the Sinai chain towered over everything else around it, so the time Moses spent there not only dominated the wilderness years, but influenced the entire lives of the Israelites and would continue to be the keystone for their descendants. According to His promise to Moses, the Lord God led His people to the place of the burning bush. He meant for them to be there a long while, to learn to worship Him in precise reverence and in praise-filled joy—and to live in a manner totally pleasing to Himself, totally designed for the well-being of the people.

They were glad to stop traveling, for it had been three months since they left Egypt. Progress was tediously slow because of the number of people: 600,000 men and their wives and children. Some of the multitude were very young, and some were very old; some were strong, some weak. And the pace for all of them was slowed further because of the browsing herds and flocks they were taking with them.

At Sinai, Moses allotted a space 50 feet by 50 feet for each family's camp and the same amount of space for their animals. It required a ten-mile square. The Lord God provided daily manna and water. The multitude lived comfortably with all their needs—if not all their wants—satisfied.

Early in their stay at Sinai Moses was reunited with his wife, Zipporah, and sons, Gershom and Eliezer; Jethro brought them from Madian. It had been almost a year since the family had been together. The boys were glad to see their father, and they were impressed by his status. Zipporah was glad to see him, too, but she was distressed by his status, for he worked more hours each day than the Hebrew slaves had worked.

One of his most time-consuming tasks was settling disputes among the people. In loving concern for his overworked son-in-law—and for his rather neglected daughter—Jethro suggested that Moses appoint capable, trustworthy, God-fearing men to judge the differences among the people. Moses followed his advice and appointed 70 men for that work. With the help of the 70, his mind and his time were freed from most of the bickering that went on between individuals, families and tribes.

But the encampment at Sinai was far from a time of rest for Moses. During those two demanding, marvelous years he climbed again and again up that craggy mountain to meet his God.

He experienced times of fasting on that mountain—once for 40 days. And he also knew times of feasting—banqueting with the Lord God. He experienced a unique fellowship with God, such as the time he was allowed to see some of the glory of God. That Shekinah glory was so brilliant that it reflected from his own face for many days even after he left the mountain.

It was on mighty Sinai that God instructed Moses on His plans to transform the freed slaves into a nation of priests. Moses, in turn, gave God's message to the people.

First he gave them God's 10 basic laws for holy, happy, well-ordered lives. Then came specific ordinances encompassing all facets of life. He described the acceptable system of offerings and sacrifices. And he brought them the wondrous plans for the tabernacle, designed in detailed symbolic patterns—a tabernacle in which the God of Abraham, Isaac and Jacob would dwell!

There were many wonderful things to remember about the Sinai encampment, but there was one heart-wrenching experience involving such bitterness that Moses seldom mentioned it and tried not to think of it. But it was a permanent part of the nation's memory.

It began while he was on that mountain, receiving from the very hand of God the tablets of the covenant, those stones inscribed by the finger of God.

It was always a difficult transition to come down from the place of holy perfection on the mountaintop to the everyday routine of human activities and weaknesses. But this time he returned not to mundane camp routine but to disaster!

The people, disturbed because he had stayed away from them for so long, had become anxious, fretful, doubtful, depressed—rebellious against him and against the Lord God. Jewelry and gold pieces that the Egyptians had showered on them as they left Mizraim were given to be melted down—for an idol! Aaron officiated. The golden idol was cast into the image of a calf, which they called god-who-brought-you-out-of-Egypt. In willful disobedience to the basic commands of the God of Abraham, Isaac and Jacob, the people gave a flippant name to a golden calf and served the idol with orgies patterned after Egypt's licentious rituals.

With his mind still full of the vision of the holy God and with the sound of His voice still in his ears, Moses began the descent from the crest of Sinai. His blessed meeting with the Lord God had ended abruptly when he was ordered to go see to his people. Elohim had seen their idolatry. He was ready to destroy them and in their place to make of Moses himself a great nation.

Moses thought of a prince who had already given up a throne. He sought no kingdom now. He was forever the servant of the Lord God, the leader of His people and an intercessor for them. He pleaded with his Master not to cast off His people.

He began the descent, made more difficult by the two heavy stone tablets he carried—and by the debilitating emotions of anger and despair that surged through him and sapped his strength.

Moses was first assaulted by raucous voices and the wild tempo of the music. Then there was the unmistakable odor of burnt offerings. Coming closer, he saw the lewd dancing, the rampant immorality. He had not felt such wrath since the day he killed the Egyptian at Akhetaton!

He dashed the tablets to the ground, smashing them as completely as the spirit of the laws written on them had been broken by the rebels. He shouted for attention, took long strides to the center of the camp and overturned the blasphemous calf.

The revelry stopped. The people, sharply brought back to a semblance of reality, were embarrassed and afraid.

Moses ordered the golden calf to be crushed into powder and mixed with water. The celebrants were ordered to drink it. There were moanings and complainings, but the command was obeyed.

Moses stood in the gate of the camp to challenge them: "Whoever is for the Lord, come to me." The Levites, Moses' own tribe, rushed to him. They were appointed executioners. Three thousand people died. The tents of the Hebrews became places of mourning.

At dawn the next day Moses left the camp quietly and alone after telling the people that he was going to the summit of Sinai to intercede for them with the Lord God. His indignation with the people had turned to sorrow. He loved them and wanted more for them than graves in the wilderness.

In the Lord God's presence he admitted the people's great sin but asked for mercy. His passionate prayer spoke eloquently of his dedication to the deliverance of the people of God: "But now, please forgive their sin—but if not, then blot me out of the book you have written."

The Lord answered His servant that He would blot out of His book only those who had sinned against Him. The people would not be cast off; they still could claim Canaan under His irrevocable covenant with Abraham.

The recollections of the triumphs and the tumults at Mt. Sinai had flashed through his mind as he walked toward the tabernacle—the treasured tent of meeting, the Holy of Holies—first assembled at Sinai.

He passed by the entrance of the court of the tabernacle without going in; the priests were already conducting the evening sacrifice. He turned and went back toward his own tent.

Memory still tumbled over memory. He stifled a sigh as he thought of the whining Israelites complaining about their monotonous diet of manna. His sigh became audible when he recalled the deep, personal hurt of the challenge to his authority by Miriam and Aaron and of the punishment of leprosy that was inflicted because of their insubordination and criticism of his leadership. Moses had interceded again, and there had been healing—of leprosy and of the relationships between the children of Amram and Jochebed.

The 40 years of wilderness wandering had been filled with enough difficulties to bring any other leader to resign his post. But Moses' love for the people and his desire to see them at long last in their own land was constant, even when he was hard pressed and angry with them.

There had been too much needless trouble, such as the time the men grumbled because the Levites were chosen as priests. Moses smiled as he thought of the Lord God's dramatic affirmation of His choice. He instructed Moses to give a staff to a leader of each tribe. Each staff was to be inscribed with the tribal name and left in the tent of meeting overnight. The next day Aaron's rod had sprouted and budded and produced almonds! The others were still wooden staffs; the question of the priesthood was settled.

Moses' head felt heavy from the load of memories, one leading into another. Now he was almost back to his own place again, thinking of that other time the people had been given the opportunity to enter their land—at Kadesh Barnea.

He remembered the 12 men he had sent covertly to find out what lay immediately across the border and further into the land. They were gone 40 days. When they returned, 10 of them thoroughly frightened the people with reports of impenetrable high walls around fortified cities, of giants and of a rampaging river to be crossed. Two of the men, Joshua and Caleb, insisted that the Lord would give them the land, whatever the obstacles.

The people sided with the majority of the spies. They would not go in. The Lord God was moved to terrible anger, and He said to Moses, "How long will they refuse to believe in me, in spite of all the miraculous signs I have performed among them? I will strike them down with a plague and destroy them, but I will make *you* into a nation greater and stronger than they."

Moses had listened in astonishment. Then, for the third time in his life, he refused a kingdom. He prayed for his beloved, stubborn, stiff-necked people, ending with a plea: "In accordance with your great love, forgive the sin of these people, just as you have pardoned them from the time they left Egypt until now."

The Lord replied, "I have forgiven them, as you asked. Nevertheless, as surely as I live and as surely as the glory of the Lord fills the whole earth, not one of the men who saw my glory and the miraculous signs I performed in Egypt and in the desert but who disobeyed me and tested me ten times—not one of them will ever see the land I promised on oath to their forefathers. No one who has treated me with contempt will ever see it."

And the message the Lord sent to the people by his servant was

> In this desert your bodies will fall—every one of you twenty years old or more who was counted in the census and who has grumbled against me. Not one of you will enter the land I swore with uplifted hand to make your home, except Caleb son of Jephunneh and Joshua son of Nun. . . . For forty years—one year for each of the forty days you explored the land—you will suffer for your sins and know what it is like to have me against you. I the Lord have spoken.

And so the wandering had resumed, and it continued for 40 years. Now the prescribed time was ended; the older generation was dead except for Moses, Joshua and Caleb.

Even some of the new generation lay buried in graves near Mount Hor along the route to the Red Sea. They had made a forced detour to avoid the jealously guarded borders of Edom. The almost impassable mountain terrain sapped their energy and exhausted their patience. In the manner of the older generation, a few began to lash out at Moses—and at the Lord God.

"Was Egypt worse than this?"

"We're hungry for real bread. We hate this wretched food."

"We never have enough water!"

They sickened Moses. They angered the Lord. Judgment came quickly in the form of darting, venomous snakes, whose bite was like stinging fire.

In panic and pain the people forgot their former exhaustion and frustration. With no antidote for the poison or medicine to ease the pain, they cried hysterically for Moses' immediate intercession with El Shaddai. Death came quickly to several; others writhed in anguish for a long time.

God's answer to their predicament was mystifying. It required no heroic procedures, no bitter herbs, no lotions, only an exercise of childlike faith. Moses, quickly obedient to His Lord's instructions, fashioned a bronze serpent and lifted it high on a pole, calling loudly to the stricken people to look at it. That was all it involved—look at the bronze serpent and live!

The remedy for the serpents' sting was perfect in its effectiveness and simplicity. But for some it came too late, while others amazingly chose to disregard God's offer of mercy, accepting only the wrath of His judgment on their personal actions and attitudes.

Moses shook his head and sighed, wondering, as he had so many times, at the distressing number of needless, desolate graves in that plot of ground and elsewhere along the way they had come. This was not the intention of their blessed Lord God. He would have had them all safe at home long ago, enjoying the glorious, pleasant, exceedingly good land of Canaan.

But now the pillar of cloud had brought them again to the edge of the holy land. The past had been sorrowed over long enough. Moses' heart surged with joy, and his mind was at peace because the children of Abraham, Isaac and

Jacob would take the land this time. The people were ready!

As for God's plans for him, he had only to wait to be told what they were. The servant was ready, too.

—22

The Lord himself goes before you and will be with you.
Deuteronomy 31:8

Moses marked off the first day of the 11th month of the 40th year since leaving Mizraim. Their journey, including the two years at Mount Sinai, should have taken less than three years!

Still in the wilderness with the riches of Canaan unappropriated, the people were understandably excited about their approaching move to occupy the land. Moses shared their high spirits, although he knew he was barred from going in. God had ordered an alternate plan for him.

Since he could not continue guiding them after they crossed the Jordan, he decided to review with them what they should have clearly in their minds.

There was so much to say before he was separated from them that it was difficult to know how to begin. Once before he had faced a permanent parting when he had wanted to say so much but found no adequate words. He could still picture in his mind's eye his mother's cottage and the way she looked at him as he stood in her doorway, unable to give her a proper good-bye. She had said, "Remember!" Then she had added a poignant "Don't forget."

In those three words she had summoned to his mind all her patient teachings and her challenges for him to be faithful to the Lord God and to live out his convictions.

He would say more than three words to the people now, but he would use "Remember!" and "Don't forget!" to emphasize his message.

Moses' aide came to tell him that the people had assembled and were waiting for him. And so under a morning sun in the desert east of the Jordan, Moses began to speak to all Israel. His strong voice would encourage them, instruct them and review their history—beginning with Sinai.

They seemed to lean forward to hear all Moses' words that were doubly precious since his time with them now was so short. His face glowed as he restated the Lord God's great promise to His people:

> The Lord our God said to us at Sinai, "You have stayed long enough at this mountain. Break camp and advance into the hill country of the Amorites; go to all the neighboring peoples in the Arabah, in the mountains, in the western foothills, in the Negev and along the seacoast, to the land of the Canaanites and to Lebanon, as far as the great river, the Euphrates. See, I have given you this land. Go in and take possession of the land that the Lord swore he would give to your fathers—to Abraham, Isaac and Jacob—and to their descendants after them."

He reminded them that when their parents refused to obey this command and were told their opportunity was forever lost, they foolishly attempted to take the land in their own way, in their own time. Without God's blessing on their venture they were routed, demoralized and reduced to living the meager life of shepherd families in sparse wilderness pastureland—moving, moving, always moving. Their lot was the more frustrating because they were tantalized by certain knowledge of a place of milk and honey where life would have been abundantly better.

Those who listened that day knew from their fathers, and from their beloved Moses, that God means for His people to accept what He offers. They knew also that when God says no or too late, He means that, too! And a whole generation that had not yet been fully tested wondered why God's people had had such difficulty with simple things like trust and obedience since the beginning of time.

As Moses continued his farewell speech, his audience could relate to many of the places he mentioned. They knew the hill country of Edom where some of Esau's descendants had denied them passage through their land, resulting in extensive circling back and around through difficult terrain. They remembered the desert road of Moab and the Zered Valley.

Many of them had fought King Sihon's army at Jahaz and now, with Moses reminding them, they remembered the power of the Lord in that battle. The Lord God had said, "See, I have begun to deliver Sihon and his country over to you. Now begin to conquer and possess his land." And they had taken the land from Aroer and from the town in the gorge as far as Gilead!

Many also remembered the divine enabling power when they met the onslaught of King Og of Bashan, and they could recite along with Moses the words the Lord God had given them then: "Do not be afraid of him, for I have handed him over to you with his whole army and his land. Do to him what you did to Sihon king of the Amorites, who reigned in Heshbon."

When those well-trained, elaborately armed enemies were overcome and their high-walled fortifications destroyed, the Israelites took from those two kings the territory east of the Jordan from the Arnon Gorge as far as Mount Hermon—all the towns on the plateau, all of Gilead and all of Bashan as far as Salecah and Edrei, towns of Og's kingdom in Bashan.

As Moses recounted the battles and the land already taken, the tribes of Reuben and Gad and the half tribe of Manasseh felt a special pride, knowing that their own kinsmen now held those prizes as their portion of the Canaan heritage.

The sun had risen higher, but the people, accustomed to more severe desert conditions, showed no inattention. They continued to stand on the slopes of a wide, natural amphitheater listening to the familiar, thundering voice of one they could not imagine being taken from them, ever!

He had finished with reminiscing now and went on to other things. There was one God to be revered and His laws to be kept inviolate!

Hear O Israel: The Lord our God, the Lord is one. Love the Lord your God with all your heart and with all your soul and with all your strength. These commandments that I give you today are to be upon your hearts. Impress them on your children. Talk about them when you sit at home and when you walk along the road, when you lie down and when you get up. Tie them as symbols on your hands and bind them on your foreheads. Write them on the doorframes of your houses and on your gates.

They were to possess the land: "He brought us out from there to bring us in and give us the land that he promised on oath to our forefathers."

The depravity of the Canaanites and others had brought them under the judgment of God; the cup of their iniquity was full. "When the Lord your God has delivered them over to you, . . . you must destroy them totally. Make no treaty with them, and show them no mercy."

The Israelites must remember that they have a unique place in God's plan. "For you are a people holy to the Lord your God. The Lord your God has chosen you out of all the peoples on the face of the earth to be his people, his treasured possession."

But they were not to be self-righteous. "The Lord did not set his affection on you and choose you because you were more numerous than other peoples, for you were the fewest of all peoples. But it was because the Lord loved you. . . ."

Over and over Moses' theme was "Remember—don't forget!"

Only be careful, and watch yourselves closely so that you do not forget the things your eyes have seen or let them slip from your heart as long as you live. Teach them to your children and to their children after them.

Remember how the Lord your God led you all the way in the desert these forty years, to humble you and to test you in order to know what was in your heart.

Both Moses and the people were getting tired, but he still had to speak of the good land; the streams, pools and springs flowing in the valleys; the magnificent hills; the fields of wheat, barley, and meadow flowers; the vines, fig trees, pomegranates, almond groves, olive oil and honey—a land of plenty, where rocks are iron and where copper can be dug from the hills—a land that drinks rain from heaven, not from irrigation ditches—a land God cares for continually, His eyes forever on it.

And in that land the Lord God would choose a singular place for His dwelling, and the people would go there to present offerings, sacrifices, tithes and special gifts. To that place they would go for feasting, rejoicing and praising the Lord God, whose name would be there!

Moses stopped speaking for a moment. Thinking of the land he would not enter with his people had made the tears come, yet he held his head high. The people looked steadily at their redeemer from bondage, their example of faith in the Lord God and of obedience to Him, the human instrument through whom God had miraculously supplied provision and protection. He began to speak again, thinking that his next words would sound presumptuous, and yet the servant proclaimed God's prophetic message:

> The Lord said to me, ". . . I will raise up for them a prophet like you from among their brothers; I will put my words in his mouth, and he will tell them everything I command him. If anyone does not listen to my words that the prophet speaks in my name, I myself will call him to account."

Finally, he reviewed their laws, their feasts of celebration, the terms of the covenant made at Sinai, the curses of the Lord God for disobedience and His blessings for obedience.

Now each closing word was chosen with the choicest loving care: "See, I set before you today life and prosperity, death and destruction. . . . Now choose life, so that you and your children may live and that you may love the Lord your God, listen to his voice, and hold fast to him."

The formal address to the assembly was completed, and now a father talked to his children: "I am now a hundred and twenty years old and I am no longer able to lead you. The Lord has said to me, 'You shall not cross the Jordan.' The Lord your God himself will cross over ahead of you. He will destroy these nations before you, and you will take possession of their land. . . . Be strong and courageous. Do not be afraid or terrified because of them, for the Lord your God goes with you; he will never leave you nor forsake you."

Then Moses summoned Joshua and said to him in the presence of all Israel: "Be strong and courageous, for you must go with this people into the land that the Lord swore to their forefathers to give them, and you must divide it among them as their inheritance. The Lord himself goes before you and will be with you; he will never leave you nor forsake you. Do not be afraid; do not be discouraged."

Speak to that rock before their eyes and it will pour out its
water.   *Numbers 20:8*

After Moses had spoken to the people he gave
himself to another task. He would make necessary additions
to the sacred writings. The man who began his career as a
scribe in Egypt had long since become the Lord God's pen-
man. He already had taken the records that were protected
in Egypt through 400 years and, as the Lord God led him,
had written the whole story of God's dealing with His world
in sequence from the time of creation.

He also had written an account of his own life and times
and a copy of the entire law and the specifications for the
tabernacle. This painstaking procedure represented a labor
of love through the years. Now it was time to complete the
record, writing of his last days as God's servant with God's
people as the Spirit of God inspired him.

When the writing was finished, he gave the scrolls to the
sons of Levi who carried the ark of the covenant of the Lord.
They and the elders were responsible for having the entire
Law read systematically to the people after they had settled
in the land.

Moses enjoyed a feeling of accomplishment and re-
warded himself with a day of rest. Into his quiet day came
thoughts of the persons about whom he had written—Adam
and Eve; Cain and Abel; Enoch; Noah; and Shem, Ham and
Japheth. Moses was fascinated with the drama of their lives
and with their places in God's plan of things. Then came
Terah, Abraham and Sarah, Isaac and Rebekah, Jacob and
Rachel and Leah—and the 12 tribes that sprang from Jacob.
He felt they would have been right at home in his own tents;
they were his kinsmen.

Jochebed had taught him about all these people and others so effectively that it seemed as if he really knew them personally; much of the material in the sacred writings that came into his possession at the exodus was familiar to him a great many years before he was moved to record it.

And now he had made his own contribution to the history of his people and would add still more pages—as long as his life lasted. Humility blended with a little pride as he thought of succeeding generations reading of him—and of those dear to him and of the people he had given much of his life to serve. He was amazed that the Lord God had led him to write such an extensive account of his own personal life and times; it was considerably larger than any other person's entry. But then he was the one the Lord God chose to weld a nation from tribes of slaves—and it had required some doing!

He closed his eyes and thought of his writings being read in assemblies down through time. Would those who read and those who heard be aware of the devotion, the testing, the endurance and the blessings of God's people as they lived out their lives of tragedy and triumph? Would they feel a kinship with him? Would they know the Lord God better because of the testimony of the writings?

Now his work was over; it was time for him to be gathered to his fathers and to his God. *Death* seemed too harsh a word for the process of "being gathered to God." By any name, Moses didn't fear it. It would be only one last obstacle to overcome. He had trusted his Lord in every other difficulty and would trust Him in this. But not to enter Canaan— that put a choking in his throat.

He had known for a long time he wouldn't enter that dear land. It was because of one terrible moment of personal rebellion against his Lord. It happened just after Miriam died and was buried by the wayside in the formidable desert of Zin. He and the bereaved Hur and Aaron were still grieving.

The people supposed that since they were caught up in private mourning, they had failed to notice that the water supply was diminishing. When it completely dried up, they blamed Moses, as they were accustomed to doing. This time the whole community met to protest.

"If only we had died when our brothers fell dead before the Lord!"

"Why did you bring us into this desert? Was it that we and our stock should die here?"

"Why did you bring us up out of Egypt to this terrible place?"

"It has no grain or figs, grapevines or pomegranates."

"And there is no water to drink!"

Suddenly it seemed to Moses that he had heard their complaints and accusations too many times! He resented their disturbing his period of mourning. He resented them! But he met their ranting with regal silence.

He and Aaron went to the tent of meeting and knelt. Soon the glory of the Lord appeared to them; there was healing, peace and calm in that glory—but Moses was too distraught to let it saturate his mind and heart. Instead, he thought of the people. He was tired of their noise!

The blessed Voice spoke to the weary servant, offering the solution to the crisis. "Take the staff, and you and your brother Aaron gather the assembly together. Speak to that rock before their eyes and it will pour out its water."

Moses and Aaron sent messengers to call the community to a special meeting in front of the designated rock. They would see for themselves how God had already provided for each one! He knew they would come. They always were eager to see signs and wonders. But when would they learn to trust God in time of need? When would they stop blaming him for their problems? Yes! They would come to the meeting; they would rejoice to have their needs met. But when they had a problem tomorrow, would they remember today? Would they ever, ever keep their mind centered on all the Lord had done for them—and all He covenanted yet to do? Would they learn to fill a burdened heart with an awareness of His glory and power and love? They had short memories and weak faith! They were more than he could bear!

He looked around at the assembly in anger. "Listen, you rebels, must we bring you water out of this rock?" His tone implied, "*We* do everything for you—and I am tired of it."

Rage clouded his soul and overshadowed his remembrance of the Lord God's precise words, "Speak to the rock . . ."

Moses raised his staff high, brandished it for a moment, then struck the rock—hard—twice.

Water gushed from it. The community and their livestock drank. Moses heard the sounds of happy people—enjoying, praising, free of the tension that had almost driven them mad a few hours before. But Moses stood still, as though made of the same substance as the stone from which the water flowed. He stared at the staff, still held in a rigid, tightly clenched fist.

Years before, when he struck the rock at Rephidim at the Lord God's instruction, he had been acutely conscious of the presence of the Lord God by that rock; he had experienced a chilling awe, for as he slashed that rock, it seemed he had slashed that unseen One at the same time. In some unexplainable way, securing the life-giving water was costly to God.

In whatever way He had been involved at Rephidim, it was not necessary that He be involved the same way again. And so this time He had told Moses only to "speak" to the rock. The second rending of it was not just a simple infraction of an arbitrary rule; it was an emotionally charged flaunting of God's own Word regarding the source of life-sustaining water.

As the community splashed in the clear-flowing water, Moses' eyes brimmed with stinging tears. His restiveness toward the people had caused him to rebel against his God. He listened without comment to the Lord's stern edict: "Because you did not trust in me enough to honor me as holy in the sight of the Israelites, you will not bring this community into the land I give them."

The punishment was severe, but God had entrusted Moses with so much power and wisdom, with so many abilities and opportunities, that He demanded much of him.

The waters there were named Meribah, which means "quarreling."

It was time to put away all the memories—of Egypt, Midian, Sinai, even Meribah. It was time to stop longing for Canaan. It was time for the Lord God to call His servant home. His holy, joyous, enervating voice spoke softly: "Now the day of your death is near." Spoken by the Lord God, those words held no terror.

Then the Voice commanded Moses: "Call Joshua and present yourselves at the tent of meeting, where I will commission him."

——————————————————————————————————————*24*

May the favor of the Lord our God rest upon us; establish the work of our hands for us—yes, establish the work of our hands.
Psalm 90:17

The servant walked with his successor toward the center of the camp, the site of the tabernacle. This would be the last time he would walk through this earthly habitation of the living God. The anticipation of it stirred his heart as much as had his first inspection of the finished tabernacle.

Even building the tabernacle had provided a thrilling experience for him—and for all Israel. The people gave generously to adorn this house of God from the treasures brought with them from Egypt. They brought in so much gold, silver, bronze, byssus and spun yarn, dyes, olive oil, spices and precious stones that Moses had to tell them to stop bringing in their offerings. There was more than enough!

Bezalel and Oholiab were the God-chosen craftsmen placed in charge. They personally transformed the priceless materials into the Lord God's grand design and instructed other workmen in the excellent way all work must be done for the tabernacle.

As Moses and Joshua walked toward the rectangular outer court's encompassing hangings of pure white byssus, the desert sun glinted on the silver fillets and bronze pins and on the bronze and silver that ornamented the acacia-wood pillars. The tabernacle's only entrance—on the eastern side—was in sight.

Moses' mind raced ahead to a hallowed place where he and Joshua would not walk on this day, the Holy of Holies where only he and the high priest were allowed to go. The remembrance of its sacred perfection filled his thoughts in an instant.

The ark of the covenant was there. The ark, made of acacia wood and covered inside and out with pure gold, held treasures from Moses' life of serving the Lord God—a golden pot of manna, Aaron's rod of almond wood that had budded, and the tablets of the law. The ark's solid gold covering was called *kaporeth*, "the propitiation," and was of one piece with the fine gold cherubim that overshadowed it, their faces turned toward the mercy seat. On the Day of Atonement each year the high priest sprinkled blood from the atonement offering on the golden kaporeth—significantly placing it between the ark below, with God's immutable law, and the pure Shekinah glory of God that filled the room above it.

Moses had longed to share the beauty of this place with all his people. He had ached to have them know the unique fellowship with the Lord God that was possible only there. To know that sweet communion with the Spirit of God was to know life and love and hope and joy beyond words!

Moses and Joshua had come to the curtained opening on the east side. Moses' strong right hand gently touched the embroidery—red, blue and purple worked into a lavish design on the white background. Through that gateway they entered the outer court.

It was quiet in this time between the morning and evening sacrifices, but the never-extinguished fire flamed on the bronze altar, and the shining bronze instruments used to prepare the sacrifices stood ready. The huge laver for cleansing the hands and feet of the priests before they entered the Holy Place was filled and waiting for use.

The servant and his aide prepared to go from the outer court into the tent of meeting. Its gateway was guarded by five acacia-wood pillars covered with gold, set in bronze and topped with capitals of gold. Over the gateway were white curtains more wondrously embroidered than those that opened into the court. In silent companionship Moses and Joshua went into the tent of meeting.

Rays of light from the seven oil-nourished flames of the beaten gold candlestick bathed the golden incense altar and the golden table with the bread of the Presence and bowls of powdered incense. The room was warmed by the light.

At that moment from the entrance to the tent of meeting streamed the Shekinah glory, proclaiming the presence of the almighty, holy God of Israel.

There was a timelessness about the moment, a settling into the atmosphere of eternity. They were at one with a pervading essence of blessing and peace and wholeness.

The Lord God spoke, and His first words were to Moses. They were personal, comforting and expected: "You are going to rest with your fathers . . ."

But the Voice continued—with a message that broke the heart of the One who spoke the words and devastated the ones who listened:

> . . . and these people will soon prostitute themselves to the foreign gods of the land they are entering. They will forsake me and break the covenant I made with them. On that day I will become angry with them and forsake them; I will hide my face from them, and they will be destroyed. Many disasters and difficulties will come upon them, and on that day they will ask, "Have not these disasters come upon us because our God is not with us?" And I will certainly hide my face on that day because of all their wickedness in turning to other gods.
>
> Now write down for yourselves this song and teach it to the Israelites and have them sing it, so that it may be a witness for me against them. . . . I know what they are disposed to do, even before I bring them into the land I promised them on oath.

The song spoke of blessings and vengeance, of sin and atonement, of difficulties, rebellion—and a faithful God.

Moses and Joshua were shaken by the song they had written as the Lord God gave the words, and they left the tent of meeting as they had entered it—in silence.

Moses noted especially a phrase that spoke of rejecting "the Rock his Savior"—and remembered Meribah. Joshua thought of the prophecy of apostasy and disasters and wondered if it would be worth the effort to take the land!

They struggled with the hard sayings but rejoiced that the song went on to state that after the wrath, the Lord God would have compassion on his servants. The last crescendo of the song carried that message:

> Rejoice, O nations, with his people,
> for he will avenge the blood of his servants;
> he will take the vengeance of his enemies
> and make atonement for his land and people.

The two men knew that the Lord God's words were infallible. Moses, relieved by his Master from the burden of the Israelites, now committed them and all their future days to the Lord God's unfailing love. Joshua, picking up that burden, also trusted the people to His redeeming love. For each of these men, serving the Lord God was their chief delight; leading the people was their means of service.

The next days were spent teaching the congregation God's great anthem. Some sang it by rote, not realizing what the words meant. Some sang with a feeling of heaviness and a tendency to give up because of the message that their future would be dismal much of the time even after crossing the Jordan. But a few sang with determination that whatever happened, they and their house would serve the Lord, would claim His promises of healing and atonement—in Canaan or wherever else they might be. The Lord God's heart was blessed by the singing of His faithful remnant.

As Moses directed the massive choir in long rehearsals, he thought of two songs he had written. One of them, 40 years before, had told of riders and horses cast into the sea and of God's provision for His redeemed people. The other song, written many years later, praised the Lord for being the dwelling place of Israel through all generations. Words from that song thrilled his heart again in the light of God's latest prophecy of tribulation:

> Make us glad for as many days as you have afflicted us,
> for as many years as we have seen trouble.

Moses' rich voice sang the old psalm, then was occupied in prayer that God's favor would rest on Israel, that the work of Israel's hands would be established.

He had not planned to address the people formally again after his very long speech to them in which he reviewed their history and reminded them of the legacy they should treasure. But now he must call them into session again and speak to them as God had ordered him to do.

This time he wouldn't talk of the past or of their heritage as God's chosen people. This time he would recite the sobering anthem he had already taught them.

It was difficult for Moses to say the harsh words, but he faithfully delivered his Master's entire message. He prophesied of corruption, shame and foolishness—and of the people abandoning the God who had made them. He spoke of the Rock who was their Savior. The message told of God's reaction of anger—and of His turning to another people to make them envious. Tears streamed down the weathered cheeks of the servant as he sounded the warning of calamities and judgments.

He paused to regain control of his voice, then raised his arms toward the heavens. His voice took on a new, resounding cadence as he spoke the last words of the anthem with joy and assurance that "atonement for his land and people" would at last come from almighty God.

The words of the anthem given to Moses by the Lord God had been spoken; they had been previously memorized by each adult. Each person knew that the Lord God had spoken to them—individually and as a nation—of judgment, but of judgment undergirded with mercy.

There remained time now for Moses to give a blessing to each tribe and words of benediction to all the people. His final words were designed to restore their eagerness to move into Canaan as the Lord God had commanded them:

Take to heart all the words I have solemnly declared to you this day, so that you may command your children to obey carefully the words of this law. They are not just idle words for

you—they are your life. By them you will live long in the land
you are crossing the Jordan to possess.

Moses looked around at the multitude—the durable, te-
nacious people he loved. Then his eyes rested on Joshua.
Joshua and the leaders who would come after him would
be hard pressed, as he had been, by the sins of these willful
people—these people who remained the apple of God's eye!
He also knew that Joshua and all future leaders could have
the Lord God's power to sustain them as they relied on Him.

That same day the Lord told Moses to go up into the
Abarim Range in Moab to Mount Nebo. From there he would
have a panoramic view of Canaan. The climb was not difficult for Moses. He who had climbed the much higher
Mount Sinai many times found Mount Nebo no problem.
His strength was not gone, and his eyes were not weak. So
he climbed to meet the Lord God and to see the beautiful
land. He viewed all of it—from Gilead to Dan, all of Naphtali,
the territory of Ephraim and Manasseh, all the land of Judah
as far as the western sea, the Negev and the whole region
from the Valley of Jericho as far as Zoar.

And Moses, the servant of the Lord, died there in Moab,
as the Lord had said. The Lord God Himself tended to the
burial of His faithful servant.

Moses had practiced being aware of the vibrant presence
of God for a long, long time. Now, with Him in a more
exhilarating way then ever before, that blessed practice
would be perfected!

Epilog

Moses said, "The Lord your God will raise up for you a prophet like me from among your own people; you must listen to everything he tells you." — Acts 3:22.

. . . the song of Moses the servant of God and the song of the Lamb:

"Great and marvelous are your deeds, Lord God Almighty.

Just and true are your ways, King of the ages.

Who will not fear you, O Lord, and bring glory to your name?

For you alone are holy.

All nations will come and worship before you,

for your righteous acts have been revealed."

—Revelation 15:3,4

Part Three

The Prophet

Moses had been enabled by God to be a miracle worker, healer, intercessor and Israel's deliverer from Mizraim. He was God's prophet, and his life was designed by God as a prophecy of the One who was to come.

Down through the centuries Israelites spoke of Moses as though he were still with them, as much a part of their lives as their contemporary judges, kings or priests.
"Moses says . . ." was the highest authority!

They entered the land under Joshua's leadership but did not obey God's command to destroy utterly those nations on whom He had pronounced judgment because of their unrepentant, idolatrous depravity. Even worse, as God prophesied through Moses, the Israelites themselves lapsed into idolatry. And so, having broken fellowship with their Protector, they endured bitter wars against invading armies and suffered devastating civil wars. Their country was divided; the northern kingdom of Israel later was forcibly dispersed into Assyria, and the southern kingdom of Judah went into a 70-year captivity in Babylon.

God restored them to their land, but in time they became estranged from Him again, demoralized and depressed. They were constantly harassed by nations coveting their strategic land and by factions within their own borders.

The Peace of Rome

At the height of the Roman empire the Jews were harshly subdued and heavily taxed by Rome. Now called Palestine, the land of Canaan was merely one of Rome's 43 provinces. That empire's nearly 50,000 miles of highways had crossroads in Palestine—a major one at Megiddo.

Their land was overrun by Gentiles. They had neither Jewish judge nor Jewish king to rule over them. Judea was governed by Rome's appointee, Herod the Idumean; Jews called him Herod the Edomite, using the ancient name for Esau's people. History has designated him Herod the Great. There were two philosophies rampant among the people—one of submission to despair, the other of anarchy against all ruling powers. Neither was God's plan for them.

Herod the Great's building program was reminiscent of that of Rameses. He, like Pharaohs of ancient times, determined to be remembered in the land he ruled. He erected elaborate buildings, palace fortresses, amphitheaters, gymnasiums, public baths, racing stadiums, even entire new cities. All this made the taxes soar and changed the looks of the beautiful land. And it influenced the life-style of the people in a way that greatly concerned the older generation of Jews, especially the Hasidim.

In Jerusalem itself Herod built an elegant fortress-palace and named it Antonia. It adjoined the temple, which Herod had completely rebuilt according to the new Hellenistic-Roman style of architecture, adding massive new walls, columns and terraces.

Yet to the most devout Jews, neither Rome's cruel oppression nor the humiliation of being ruled by a descendant of Esau was as heavy a burden as the realization that the prophecy Moses had given them from the Lord God in his last "song" had come to pass. The people had prostituted themselves to foreign gods. God had become angry with them.

Surely God had hidden His face for a very long time. It had been more than 400 years since the prophet Malachi told them of His displeasure over the corruption of their priests, the sins of the people and the stinginess of their offerings to Him.

But they had reason to hope! Malachi also spoke of the "messenger of the covenant" who was yet to come. There were many in Palestine who looked for—longed for—that promised One, as their fathers in Egypt after 400 years of bondage had looked for someone to redeem them.

Abimael and Hadoram left the Nazareth synagogue one very warm spring evening and began the long walk to the house of Heli and Anna. Their minds were filled with the words of prophecy the rabbi had read and with the substance of the lengthy discussion that followed the reading. Each felt the topic was too deep. Hillel himself would not be able to explain it adequately, much less the Galilean peasants.

Still, it had been interesting, and each had an opinion of what the prophets meant.

They were oblivious to the moonlight that gave the town square delicate shadings of light and dark. The square was quiet. Open-air markets were folded away for the night; the old men who daily sat around exchanging memories and advice were home in bed.

Abimael and Hadoram followed the dusty street up the long, steep grade to where Heli's house stood in a cluster of one-story mud-brick houses on the side of the hill.

"Heli keeps his house in good repair. New lattices on the front window, I see." Hadoram found it comfortable to speak of everyday things, pushing overwhelming thoughts away temporarily.

"Yes. Looks nice. But that means his business is slow, for if there's work to be done for pay he will do that first. This might be a good time to have him make me a new winnowing shovel." The younger of the two also found it a welcome diversion to speak of minor matters.

They climbed the wooden ladder to the roof of the house. Straw mats were spread for the guests, and Heli was waiting for them—eager to hear what was said at the synagogue that evening.

"Shalom, Abimael and Hadoram, my friends—and a long life."

"And peace to you, Heli, and to your wife, Anna." They answered almost in unison.

"Please, sit down." Heli motioned to the mats with the graciousness of a host offering the finest leather cushions. And the guests, tired from their busy work day, the long meeting at the synagogue and the uphill walk, sat down and smiled as though experiencing luxurious ease.

Heli poured a small cup of wine for his guests and himself, then gave them a moment to catch their breath. He sipped his wine slowly, trying to hide his impatience. Then he made a start at getting to what he wanted to hear. "I see you got the message I sent with Joel, and I thank you for coming. I know you would rather have gone home at this late hour."

Hadoram answered, "Yes. Joel told us Anna is ill and you thought it best not to leave her and Miriam tonight. I trust she is resting better now."

"Yes, she's more comfortable. Miriam stays with her." Heli relaxed and smiled at the sound of the name of his well-loved daughter. "Miriam is grown into a dependable young woman, loving and happy—the joy of our lives.

"But, tell me. What of the meeting? You did continue to search the Scriptures for prophecies of Messiah the Prince?"

"Yes!" Abimael's excitement was evident in his voice.

Hadoram picked up the conversation. "The rabbi read again from the scrolls—the prophecies of One to be born of a virgin, in Bethlehem of Judea, from the tribe of Judah, house of David—the same writings of Isaiah, Micah and Samuel we read and discussed at our last meeting. You remember that rather heated discussion last time, Heli, especially the argument about the improbability—some say impossibility—of Isaiah really meaning that the Sent One would be born of a virgin!"

Heli interrupted his guest with an impatient wave of his hand. "If you continued with that, I'm glad I wasn't there. There's no point in arguing about that beyond a reasonable point. We can't explain it; we can't comprehend it. It's as Moses says, 'The secret things belong to God.' "

"Heli . . ." Hadoram spoke as though his host were a child. His studied patience irritated rather than calmed the atmosphere. ". . . as I told you, we only *read* those passages again—as background—then we went on to other prophecies."

Hadoram stopped to savor what he was about to share with Heli. "My friend, it's a coincidence that you just spoke of Moses. We talked of him all evening."

"Talked of Moses? You studied the Law, not the Prophets?"

Hadoram raised his voice to give an unmistakable signal that he was weary of interruptions. "We talked of *Moses!* In particular, we talked of the *prophecy* God gave him concerning the *Prophet* He would send—One who would be like Moses. Hear the very words! Anyone who did not already know them would have memorized them tonight!"

The Lord said to me: "I will raise up for them a prophet like you from among their brothers; I will put my words in his mouth, and he will tell them everything I command him. If anyone does not listen to my words that the prophet speaks in my name, I myself will call him to account."

They observed a customary silence after speaking the words of the Lord, then Hadoram continued: "For the rest of the time we considered signs to watch for in order to be able to recognize the coming One—this One like Moses."

Hadoram smiled, noticing the effect his words were having on Heli. He finally held his friend's eager attention.

"We decided that since there were such very dramatic prophecies about events at the birth of the coming One, God must have wanted us to know who He was from the very beginning of His lifetime. If so, we should be able to find similarities between Him and Moses, even in—especially in—infancy."

Heli jumped up, paced in anger, then turned to shake his finger at Hadoram. "Everyone knows Moses had a normal birth—in Egypt—and was of the tribe of Levi. Your analogy is broken. Why go on with these . . . these unedifying tangents?"

"*Because!*" Hadoram spoke as if that were defense enough. Then he went on, "Because we believe no man, not even Moses, will have *all* the credentials of Messiah. The prophecy was that he would be 'like'—not 'exactly like'! I am trying to tell you: We studied to see if there are any signs around Moses' birth that are similar to what we could expect at Messiah's birth. Sit down, Heli, and consider: The king of the land where Moses was born was an unprecedented builder—at the expense of the very lives of many of his slaves."

"I do consider Herod a wild man when it comes to building, but we are not slaves, Hadoram; we are free!"

"Free? Free to pay such heavy taxes there is no more left as a reward for our labor than if we were slaves. But . . .

please, hear me out! Moses came when the tribes of Jacob were under Gentile oppression—and when it had been more than 400 *years* since the Lord God had spoken to His people."

Heli sat down, remembering his role as host to invited guests. He tried to respond to Hadoram without the sting in his voice. "Interesting . . . an interesting coincidence to our present situation."

"Coincidence?" Now the sting was in young Abimael's voice; he fairly spit out that word. "One or two coincidences would not be worthy of consideration. We are talking of the whole pattern of a life from beginning to end—a pattern to help us recognize our Messiah! You said you were glad you weren't at the meeting tonight; I'm glad, too! If you had been there, we would never have covered the subject as we did. Now, you asked us to come here to tell you what we learned from tonight's study. Hear all of it before you decide we are indulging in tangents and coincidences!"

Heli shrugged his shoulders. "I will try to listen, but it seems unlikely that Herod would bother killing Jewish babies as Pharaoh killed male children in Egypt; he's too busy murdering political enemies and his royal family."

Hadoram's voice thundered in rage, *"Royal?* That Edomite usurper? That turncoat?"

"I didn't mean to upset you. I won't mention him again, except to say that *if* Herod did despise Jewish babies that much, according to *your* theory, his mother would have to put her endangered infant in an ark and set him adrift on the Jordan, since we don't have a Nile." Heli laughed softly at his word picture, then felt uneasy for having laughed.

His friend treated his taunt seriously. "It's possible that if God wanted to draw certain parallels between Moses and Messiah, He might arrange that He sleep, as a baby, in an unusual cradle and have a lovely Miriam watch over him. It would be a fascinating way to mark an early similarity. It would be a certain sign. Wouldn't you agree?"

"Oh, I suppose so, but it's too unlikely; we are still wasting time. Get to the adult life of Moses. Enough talk of infants!"

"Well, my cousin Joel mentioned early in our meeting

that he was impressed that Moses gave up the riches of Egypt to identify with a slave people. He thinks Messiah may be offered a great world kingdom—maybe as great as Rome—then reject it in order to get on with the redemption of His people."

Hadoram thought he had made a strong point that should be contemplated for a while, but Abimael moved the discussion along.

"At first, the Hebrews didn't recognize Moses' greatness. Even after he showed them signs and wonders never done before, they still distrusted him. They always wanted more, more, more—and when their needs weren't met quickly and in the way they wanted, you know how they turned on Moses, even attempting a few times to kill him! I would hope our people won't be so blind when this One comes. Imagine trying to stone the Messiah!"

That was a disquieting thought, and no one wanted to comment on it. Heli changed the subject. "Do you suppose He will be a shepherd before He makes formal presentation of Himself to the people—as Moses was a shepherd in Midian?"

Hadoram slowly spoke the thoughts that filled his mind at that question. "It would seem appropriate. Abraham, Isaac and Jacob—and David—were shepherds, as well as Moses. This coming One might well be one—or He might be a symbolic shepherd. Our father Jacob was the first to give the Lord God the name of Shepherd of Israel—and David sang of our Shepherd Lord.

"Whether or not He will be an actual shepherd, He *will* be a mediator between God and man as Moses was many times. He *will* do great miracles that no one else has ever done. He *will* be a man of greatest faith and deepest prayer, and He *will* have perfect love for God and for His people."

"And do you think our people would try to kill such a One—as Abimael fears?"

"They tried to kill Moses. And important prophecies by both Isaiah and David speak of One who will suffer intensely."

Abimael decided the talk was becoming too philosophical. "We've spoken of symbolic shepherding, mediating between God and man and implied suffering . . . but there will have to be very practical tests, too. One that would convince me the Prophet was the one like Moses is that He would go for 40 days without bread or water—as Moses did when he was on Mount Sinai. That would be something a lesser prophet wouldn't want to attempt to imitate!"

All three men laughed. Abimael's enormous appetite was well known. Then, the tension of their serious conversation having been eased, they sat in comfortable silence for a time, considering what had already been said.

Heli decided to bring the long evening to a close. "You've given me some things to think about, at least. Surely none of our fathers is better known to us than Moses, and this is good. We will have much with which to compare the life of the coming One."

Abimael was preoccupied with a question that had returned to his own mind. "When this Son of David comes, we must hear Him . . . pay attention to all He says . . . for God has warned of the consequences if we don't. We need more meetings such as the one at the synagogue this evening to help us learn how to identify Him. I'm sure that since we have so many prophecies about Him, we will know who He is when He comes to us. We most certainly will not mistreat Him as our fathers mistreated Moses."

Hadoram rose to leave, still talking. "People don't change much from one generation to another—or from one era to another. Many of our people even now wouldn't recognize Him because they haven't studied the Scriptures, and many won't want to recognize Him because He will challenge old ways, even ways instituted by Moses."

"What would He change?" Abimael had risen, too, almost without realizing it, for he was intent on what his companion had just said.

"I don't know all the changes He would make, but Moses changed the system of sacrifices and introduced new rituals of worship. Israel wouldn't take it kindly if the Prophet tampered with those things."

Abimael was quick to respond, "I should think not! Our

system of sacrifice is all-encompassing, complete. Our ceremonies are more inspiring than any others that could be devised . . . at least they are when they are conducted by properly chosen priests. The Prophet can't change all that!"

"You see? People are still the same." Hadoram raised his arms to the skies in a mock despair that emphasized his point.

Abimael angrily asked, "Would you welcome a change in our temple sacrifices?"

"If . . . if One comes with a more excellent method of atonement for our sins—a God-ordained substitution for what we have now—we should be humbled with praise and thanksgiving."

"And a change of priesthood? Do you remember when, in Moses' time, others than Levites, even others than the house of Gershom, challenged the right of priests? They were cursed!"

"Abimael, the present priesthood has become a travesty, nothing more than a political reward to the Sadducee who impresses Herod the most. I think . . . I think the Promised One just might institute an entirely new priesthood—as Moses did."

"The moonlight has made you mad, Hadoram."

It was the host's turn to speak. "Thank you both for your patience and your time—and what you have shared with me about the study of the One like Moses. Even though we are ending our evening with more questions than we had before, it's good to think about such things. By the way . . . what about Pharaoh's army defeated at the Red Sea? I hope this Prophet will bring Rome down . . . and all of Israel's other enemies!"

Abimael assumed a priestly tone to parrot words he often heard his elders say: "In God's time, He will." Then, instead of allowing the conversation to wind down as the other two apparently wanted it to, he began a new line of thought. "There's a prophecy from Daniel I wanted to have read this evening, but we didn't have time in the meeting to take out another scroll. I wanted the rabbi to read Daniel's prophecy of Messiah the Prince. The 70 seven-year periods that he

said must elapse before His coming are about gone and
. . ."

". . . and just as we didn't have time for it in the synagogue, we don't have time for it now. We must go!" Hadoram ended the session.

Abimael held his head with his hands and said, "Yes,
let's go. My head throbs from trying to sort things out. But
first, Heli, I meant to ask if you would make me a winnowing
shovel."

"I think so. I have only a little work ahead now . . .
oxgoads for Amariah and a bedding chest to finish for Eder.
. . . Do you want it made of oak?"

"Yes. I want it to last."

"I'll have it ready by the time you need it."

Abimael nodded approval, then casually mentioned that
he had heard young Izhar was going to the Essenes at Qum-
ran to inquire about becoming part of their community. And
he hoped the weather would be cooler soon.

Hadoram expressed his concern about his nephew, Jehiel, who had joined the Zealots in the Galilean hills. And
he hoped they would get some rain in a few days.

Then with the traditional "Shalom," the guests left.

Miriam had gone outside the doorway just after her father's friends arrived. The house was quite warm, and she
wanted some fresh air and a refreshing look at the moonlit
sky.

She had heard her father say, "Miriam's with her . . .
Miriam is dependable." She sighed with the patient indulgence the young often have for the older generation. She
had tried to persuade him to call her Mary, as those of her
own age did, but he and her mother kept to the old form
of her name. She admired Miriam, who had watched over
a helpless infant in Egypt, but she still preferred to be called
Mary.

Mary was glad her father's friends had come. They would
take his mind off his ailing wife; he worried too much about
her. He and his friends enjoyed lively conversations—usually about disagreements over the interpretation of points of

Scripture. They challenged each other's viewpoints, upheld their own convictions—and still always parted as friends.

Their voices sounded more intense than usual this evening. She walked around to where she could hear them better. When she learned that their conversation was about the longed-for Messiah, she listened closely.

She already knew the things they were saying—that He would be of the tribe of Judah and of the house of David. She had been taught that ever since she could remember. But her heart sang when she heard it said again with the sound of excitement—as though it were imminent! The Messiah would be for all the people, but He would be her near kinsman! She of the house of David felt fortunate.

Just then her mother called, and she went into the house to attend her. It was much later when she went back outside. She wanted to hear every word about Messiah's coming, but she missed almost the entire discussion.

And she could make no sense of what the men were saying when she picked up their conversation again. Someone might change the system of sacrifice and the ceremonial rituals! Some new Prophet of God, they were saying. But she could imagine that most of the Jews would consider such a one a blasphemer or a lunatic. She couldn't imagine what had led up to that incomprehensible conversation. She wished she hadn't heard any of it. A new kind of Prophet—a new order.

Well, such were things the elders talked about. And even Hadoram, Abimael and her father didn't seem too concerned about it all, for—unbelievably—their talk had turned to shovels and the weather, to Essenes and Zealots!

Mary felt a certain sadness for her father and his friends. They talked of such high things—and believed them—but were caught in the web of daily pressures to make a living. And she wondered about Izhar and Jehiel, trying in opposite ways to hasten what could come only in the fullness of time—God's time.

As the men called out "Shalom" and walked toward the ladder, Mary hurried back into the house.

Until she went to sleep late that night, she thought of

that conversation of which she had heard snatches—that amazing conversation. She could hardly wait to go to the well the next morning to tell whoever was there what the rabbi and the congregation had been talking about.

Then she would try to find Joseph and tell him, too. The future they planned together just might be blessed and marvelously enriched because, some thought, it was time for Him to come—the Prophet like Moses.

And even though she couldn't understand what it all meant, in the simplicity of her faith she knew it meant—everything!

She hoped He would come quickly!

* * * * *

MARANATHA!

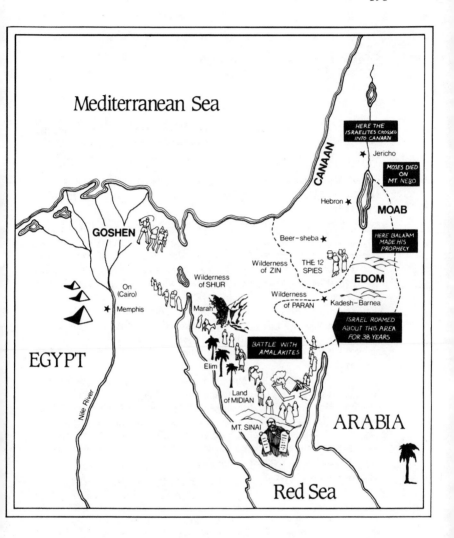

CHRISTIAN HERALD ASSOCIATION AND ITS MINISTRIES

CHRISTIAN HERALD ASSOCIATION, founded in 1878, publishes The Christian Herald Magazine, one of the leading interdenominational religious monthlies in America. Through its wide circulation, it brings inspiring articles and the latest news of religious developments to many families. From the magazine's pages came the initiative for CHRISTIAN HERALD CHILDREN and THE BOWERY MISSION, two individually supported not-for-profit corporations.

CHRISTIAN HERALD CHILDREN, established in 1894, is the name for a unique and dynamic ministry to disadvantaged children, offering hope and opportunities which would not otherwise be available for reasons of poverty and neglect. The goal is to develop each child's potential and to demonstrate Christian compassion and understanding to children in need.

Mont Lawn is a permanent camp located in Bushkill, Pennsylvania. It is the focal point of a ministry which provides a healthful "vacation with a purpose" to children who without it would be confined to the streets of the city. Up to 1000 children between the age of 7 and 11 come to Mont Lawn each year.

Christian Herald Children maintains year-round contact with children by means of a *City Youth Ministry*. Central to its philosophy is the belief that only through sustained relationships and demonstrated concern can individual lives be truly enriched. Special emphasis is on individual guidance, spiritual and family counseling and tutoring. This follow-up ministry to inner-city children culminates for many in financial assistance toward higher education and career counseling.

THE BOWERY MISSION, located at 227 Bowery, New York City, has since 1879 been reaching out to the lost men on the Bowery, offering them what could be their last chance to rebuild their lives. Every man is fed, clothed and ministered to. Countless numbers have entered the 90-day residential rehabilitation program at the Bowery Mission. A concentrated ministry of counseling, medical care, nutrition therapy, Bible study and Gospel services awakens a man to spiritual renewal within himself.

These ministries are supported solely by the voluntary contributions of individuals and by legacies and bequests. Contributions are tax deductible. Checks should be made out either to CHRISTIAN HERALD CHILDREN or to THE BOWERY MISSION.

Administrative Office: 40 Overlook Drive, Chappaqua, New York 10514
Telephone: (914) 769-9000